Best wishes,

Brian Statham.

Bowled Statham

The Authorized Biography

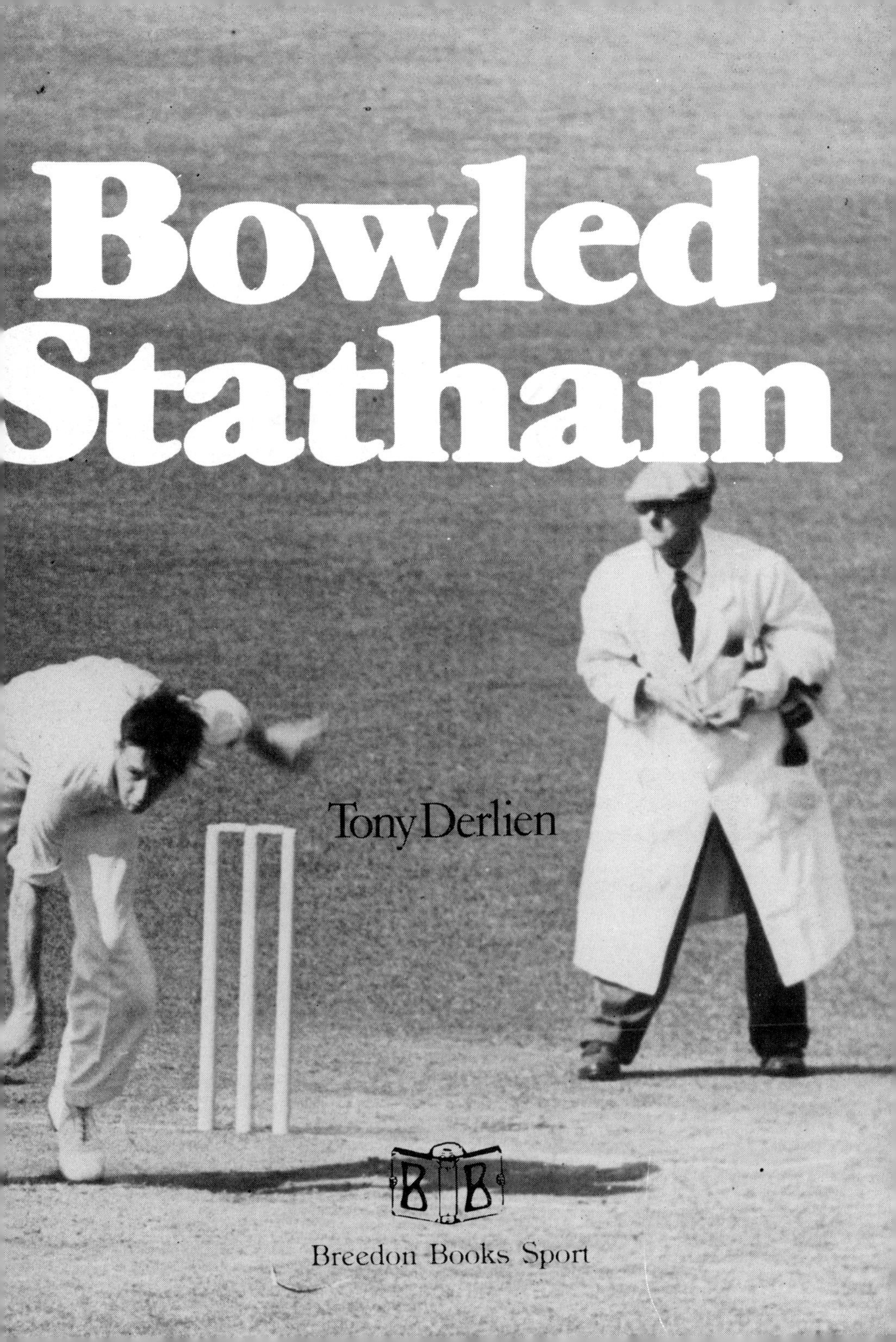

Bowled Statham

Tony Derlien

Breedon Books Sport

First published in Great Britain by
The Breedon Books Publishing Company Limited
44 Friar Gate, Derby DE1 1DA
1990

ISBN 0 907969 75 5

Printed by Butler and Tanner Limited, Frome, Somerset.
Jacket designed by Graham Hales and printed by Arkle Press Ltd, Northampton.

Contents

Preface

THE story of Brian Statham's career deserves telling. Fred Trueman, his partner in half his Tests, reckons "there is no doubt that Brian was the most accurate quick bowler who has ever played cricket."

Certainly, Statham's bowling average of 16.36 is the lowest of *any* post-1918 player who has taken over 2,000 wickets; and the lowest of *any* post-1945 player who has taken even 1,000 wickets. Furthermore, he conceded only 2.2 runs per over, an economy seldom bettered (notably by Maurice Tate's 2.00).

Since retirement Statham has rarely been in the limelight, whereas Trueman has rarely been out of it. This book will help to restore the balance, as Fred himself did last year by organizing two testimonial dinners for his partner, who has been unlucky in recent years.

My chief thanks go to Brian Statham, for his long-standing approval of my text and for his Foreword.

My thanks also go to the staff of Manchester Central Reference Library, whose comprehensive newspaper records were indispensable at every stage.

Tony Derlien
May 1990

Foreword
by Brian Statham

LAST year, Fred Trueman arranged a Dinner for my benefit — and partly for charity, too. He knew that I was unemployed and had developed osteoporosis and it was typical of him to think of giving me a boost.

Unlike Fred, I'd been out of the limelight for 20 years, so it was quite an occasion for me to meet so many of my former teammates. The talk flowed at every table, recalling the cricket of the 1950s and 1960s.

I was lucky enough then to play in 70 Tests and 430 matches for Lancashire— but far be it from me to tell you which records I broke. This book will tell you, though, because it tells you about everything I achieved on the cricket field. As you can see from the chapter headings, Tony Derlien describes all the highlights of my career in full detail.

My own most vivid memories include my dramatic first Roses match; my Test debut the very next winter; my partnership with Frank Tyson in Australia; my successful Lord's Test of 1955; my three hat-tricks; my two 15-wicket match hauls, plus a 14 and a 13; my (briefly!) world record-breaking 237th Test wicket; my appointment as Lancashire captain in 1965, which was also one of my best-ever bowling seasons; my CBE; my breaking of Johnny Briggs' Lancashire bowling records (not that I realized at the time!); and my dramatic farewell match in 1968.

I would like to take this opportunity to thank my colleagues for their friendship throughout my career, and also the general public who so willingly paid at the gate to watch us. I am especially grateful, of course, to everyone who supported my Benefit in 1961.

Finally, I am grateful to my wife and family for adjusting so well to my hectic life as a cricketer.

Brian Statham
May 1990

The Way to Old Trafford

BORN at Gorton, near Manchester, on 17 June 1930 and the youngest of four brothers, John Brian Statham was never coached as a bowler, although in view of his achievements, it is fair to assume that he did not need to be, in the way that Sir Jack Hobbs never received coaching as a batsman.

True, Brian Statham was given advice in his early days, but this is not to say that it was necessarily beneficial, nor that he decided to follow it. In other words, he was a 'natural' bowler, not because his parents or grandparents were skilful at games. Indeed, not for any particular reason. It was probably just that he must have found at school, where he was an all-round sportsman, that his loose-limbed, elastic-muscled body made fast bowling a rewarding and relatively effortless pursuit.

There is a parallel between Statham's suppleness and that of Ted McDonald, Lancashire's earlier world-class fast bowler. McDonald could clasp his hands together in front of him and take them up over his head and, still clasped, down his back to reach his waistline.

Statham could perform a similar feat. And he could remove his sweater by reaching down his back to the hem and pulling it up over his shoulders. He could, as a party trick, put his right arm behind his head, then under his chin and so tickle his right ear. In a nutshell, both Statham and McDonald were what is popularly known as 'double-jointed'.

When I say that Statham found fast bowling relatively effortless, I mean compared to the effort others would have needed to make to achieve as much (such as 96 wickets at three runs apiece for his RAF station at a time when, aged 19, he was not even actively seeking a cricket career); or to the effort he would have needed to make to become a famous batsman. I do not mean that he worked short of his hardest at the job in hand; perhaps I simply mean that he chose the task at which his effort was the most productive.

His eldest brother was a local league fast bowler and, although he did not see him play at that level, by the time he entered primary school, Brian had picked up an ambition to be a fast bowler himself. Yet, strangely, this ambition long remained latent and never cut across his talents or enthusiasm for other sports until he was 17 — and even then he had no thought of first-class cricket until it was suggested to him two years later still.

Brian played both cricket and soccer a great deal throughout his childhood and youth, at first on a cinder-covered wasteland, on which it was useless for a bowler to allow the ball to pitch on the way to the stumps. Perhaps his future disinclination to bowl short and his fine control of the yorker stemmed from this.

I think it is fair to say that Statham played soccer more continuously, and to a higher standard, than he played cricket in the period before he reached 17. And there were summers when his enthusiasm for tennis shut out cricket.

In his first year at Manchester Central High School in Whitworth Street he was chosen for the Under-14 XI at both soccer and cricket. In the next school year he played for the Second XI cricket team, but outside school he played only soccer. When he reached the school First XI at cricket he became disillusioned because, although the headmaster and the sportsmaster were very encouraging to all the teams, he was a small fish forced into the background by the prefects and by boys who were good enough to play local league cricket.

So, by the time he left school at 16 he had lost interest in cricket — to the extent of playing tennis practically every evening. His keenness on soccer, on the other hand, did not flag and his standard was such that his left-wing partner for the local Denton West club was Roger Byrne, who later became an England international player with Manchester United.

First Division scouts were interested in teams of this standard but when those from Manchester United watched Denton West, Statham was missing owing to an injury. Nevertheless, he was seen and offered trials by no less than Manchester City, Liverpool, Stockport and Bury — trials he never attended because his father, whose word to him was law, forbade it. His father, a dentist, was influenced partly by doubts about the career prospects and partly by a bad injury from amateur soccer to another of his four sons; and so, from Brian Statham's teenage team, it was left to Roger Byrne to find the heights of the soccer world and the cruel fate which was waiting there for him. Statham, turned away from soccer largely by his father, also found influences greater than his own — off the field, that is — in directing his cricket career.

The first of these was a man called Eric Taylor, who was the organizer of Denton West's soccer team and who wished to keep the boys together during the summer. He invited them to join Denton West Cricket Club, of which he was a vice-president, and many of them did so, including, of course, Brian Statham; the latter, incidentally, because he enjoyed outdoor games so much, rather than because it happened to be a cricket club.

This was a turning-point. His one-time schoolboy enthusiasm for cricket came rushing back: "I thought I had been completely happy playing soccer but, suddenly, I realized that many hours in white flannels — even though I might not take a wicket — were far more satisfying than scoring a couple of goals in 90 minutes of soccer." Of this period, he adds: "Always I have played sport for sheer enjoyment. This was particularly true during the two seasons I was with Denton West. I enjoyed bowling more than anything else, and match after match I was allowed to carry on in my own way. I never bothered about 'style'. Averages mattered even less."

This was surely, to put it into one phrase, the emergence of a natural bowler.

He was successful enough with his club to earn his first money from cricket. (Since leaving school, he had been working for an accountant and was to stay there over two years.) His 'income' from cricket came from collections which were taken amongst the crowd for, in the case of a bowler, the taking of seven wickets or a hat-trick. By once capturing eight wickets for 15 runs he earned 5s 4d!

In 1948, his second season with Denton West, when he was 18, he turned down an offer to join Stockport in the Central Lancashire League and ended that summer atop his club and the North-Western League bowling averages — the award for this was £1!

In October 1948, Statham began 18 months of National Service in the RAF, stationed as a clerk at Number 16 Maintenance Unit, Stafford. One of the first questions he was asked was about his sporting interests and he remains convinced that the Services offer first-rate opportunities for sport.

Following on where he had left off the previous summer, he retained cricket as his major sport and tennis had to be kept in second place. He also represented the station at table tennis and played soccer at a lower level.

In the summer of 1949, he dismissed 96 batsmen while bowling for his station, each wicket averaging a mere three runs. Statham says that he was helped by the pitches, which were all in his favour as long as he adjusted his sights. They were so lively that a ball pitched on a good length usually rose over the stumps. He therefore used the yorker to dismiss a large proportion of his victims.

At Stafford, the grass was fine but was laid on sand which meant that he could remove a turf by the impact of his front foot as it landed. This did not put him off — but he was very grateful that he was not a batsman there.

Statham also played in the Command Cup that year, for Maintenance Command, who progressed well. When Transport Command finally defeated them, Statham nevertheless had five wickets for his part, not to mention 30 runs. However, he did not represent the RAF itself. Had he done so, he would have come up against such players as Peter May (Navy) and Frank Tyson (Army) that summer.

It was the RAF which provided the second important influence in directing Statham's cricket career. This was Corporal Lazarus, cricket organizer at Stafford. Although he did not play the game, he was a cricket fanatic. Early in the 1949 season, Lazarus was quick to see — and probably the first to see — that Brian Statham was good enough for the first-class game.

Lazarus asked Statham whether he had thought of playing county cricket. Statham, surprised, answered honestly, "No." Statham records that until that moment he had never had a single thought of becoming a county cricketer.

The corporal, a Londoner, decided to write on the matter to MCC, partly perhaps with the aim of strengthening his favourite team, Middlesex. MCC advised him that the player should first apply to the county of his birth and it was Lazarus who also wrote off this application. It is interesting to note that Statham, off the field, played a passive role in organizing his future. When his National Service was over, his accountancy job would still be available to him and, although he would have much preferred an outdoor life, he did no more towards arranging one than simply carry on bowling. He was content to leave it to men like Lazarus, at their own discretion, to spread the news of his ability.

Lancashire responded in late June by offering a trial to Statham, who was then just 19 years old. The trial took place in early August 1949. Statham's father gave Brian permission to attend on the condition that, if engaged, he must make the grade — presumably become a first-team regular — within three years or leave.

At this stage, Brian Statham had never seen a county match and therefore decided that he had better have a look at one as soon as possible. He went to Old Trafford to see the match against Middlesex and his main impression was one of amazement at Pollard's swing bowling. Dick Pollard was Lancashire's opening bowler, even though he was almost, at the age of 37, at the end of his long and successful career. Indeed, he had no rival at Old Trafford in 1949.

Statham sat in the stand directly behind Pollard's arm and wondered how the ball was made to swing so much. He was also impressed by the large number of runs that Middlesex made, which included 207 for their first wicket (Pollard notwithstanding), compared to the all-out totals of under a hundred that had been normal in his own matches; and, taking a wide view, by how serious a business county cricket seemed to be.

A few weeks after this visit, he was given leave from the RAF to attend the trial at Old Trafford — but, ironically, it was rained off. Moreover, another trial was not possible until the new season of 1950.

It is noteworthy that Statham was led towards Old Trafford, not only by RAF cricket (via Corporal Lazarus) but also by his concurrent games for Stockport, for whom he managed to play six times in 1949, by virtue of weekend leave from his station.

Stockport, joint champions of the Central Lancashire League that season, had several links with Lancashire County Cricket Club. Stockport's Barry Howard (himself a leading Lancashire Second XI player during the week) was the brother of the Lancashire captain and the son of the 1932-1948 Lancashire secretary; Malcolm Hilton, Lancashire's spin bowler, twice deputized as the Stockport professional that summer; and Lancashire's coach, Harry Makepeace, naturally kept in touch with league matches.

The most significant of Statham's games for Stockport came a few weeks after the rained-off county trial. It was a benefit match for their professional, Wally Walmsley, an Australian leg-spinner. In his first over, Statham clean bowled another Australian, 'Jock' Livingston, with a yorker; Livingston was then a league professional and the next season he was to join Northamptonshire and score more runs than anyone else for them that year. Livingston reported back to the Lancashire coach that he had seen a bowler capable of succeeding Pollard.

Indeed, Makepeace watched Statham playing for Stockport at about this time and in April 1950 he duly sent him the promised reinvitation to a trial. Makepeace was then aged nearly 70 and had coached Lancashire players for some 20 years. Before that, starting as long ago as 1906, he had scored the rare total of over 25,000 runs, mostly as a Lancashire opening batsman.

Statham recalls that Makepeace, on meeting him at the trial, said: "I have been here a long time, lad, and it has been a happy time. Come, let's see what you can do." It may have been a well-worn greeting, but it was none the less apt for that.

The trial was basically a two-day game, each team comprising an even share-out of the various levels of the Old Trafford staff. Statham dismissed two regular first-team batsmen, Winston Place and Alan Wharton, in spite of lbw decisions not applying in the match. Makepeace was one of the game's umpires, and, of course, he also saw Statham in the nets, where the new bowler managed to hit the county secretary whilst the latter was watching from behind the stumps, the net protecting him at that point being in disrepair.

After the trial, it was decided that Statham was worthy of being taken on and he was offered terms at once. His RAF service terminated on 1 May 1950, and in mid-May he reported to Old Trafford as a professional cricketer. He spent his time bowling in the nets, not to the senior players, because their season had started, but to the Lancashire members. He also played in Club & Ground matches and was chosen for the Second XI — then the reigning Minor Counties champions — and played in their first five games, taking 26 wickets which cost 14 runs apiece.

Dick Pollard, meanwhile, played five games for the county side, although he had been dropped for the Roses match at Sheffield at the end of May. It is certain that Lancashire, with their attack abundant in spin but short of real pace, were looking for a replacement for Pollard. And if 1949 had been to some extent his year — it saw his very large benefit of £8,000 and also his 1,000th wicket for the county — then 1950 was to see his swan-song.

Statham must have been considered in this light and in mid-June, after about a month as a professional, he was selected to play for the First XI against Kent at Old Trafford, the match starting on his 20th birthday. It was Makepeace who broke the news to a surprised Statham, but the decision was more that of the First and Second XI captains, the Howard brothers, than of Makepeace. The latter understandably thought that the time was not yet ripe, but at least now he really would be able to see what Statham could do.

The Natural Bowler

WHAT could Brian Statham do? What sort of bowler had arrived — to stay — at Old Trafford? Statham says that he had always been able to bowl on the fast side compared to his peers, but some opinion, including Trevor Bailey's, has it that he was not genuinely fast in his first year in first-class cricket. As to his development of speed, I shall refer to this from time to time later.

Nor was he a lethal swing bowler. After recalling the initial impression which Pollard's bowling had made upon him in this respect, Statham adds: "In 19 seasons I never discovered how a fast bowler could swing the ball through the air at will!" He could swing the ball either way, but it went at its own sweet will. Players such as Bailey, Brian Close and Fred Trueman confirm that swing was far from being one of Statham's major weapons.

Statham's action when he was first seen by Lancashire was not highly-rated. Although he probably always had a beautifully high point of delivery, it was judged to be more ungainly than rhythmic at that time, perhaps because his then lightweight body lacked strength — his early nickname was the 'Whippet'. When his shoulders, in particular, developed, he probably had the power to control his movements more and thus produce the smooth flowing action which became greatly admired.

Statham was criticized for delivering with his chest somewhat facing the batsman rather than sideways-on to him, this in conjunction with his left arm and shoulder pointing towards the slips area rather than towards fine leg.

Thus, he eyed the batsman from inside his raised left elbow, rather than from outside, which latter position is the textbook one and the one used by nearly all the top fast bowlers of the game's history. The textbook also indicates the closely-related sideways-on chest position.

However, when this left arm and chest position was pointed out to him, Statham felt it was too late to alter it, fearing as he did the sacrifice of his accuracy for the sake of being technically correct.

Incidentally, his action contained another fault which he decided, for the same reason, not to try to eradicate. This was his landing immediately before the delivery stride on the side of his right boot instead of firmly on the whole spiked sole. It actually caused him to fall flat in various matches throughout his career — including several Tests — but, helped by managing to fall softly, he decided that his bowling as a whole would not benefit from any attempted correction.

Thus, one has so far identified, as up to a point Harry Makepeace must have done, a slim, young bowler of perhaps 'no more than ordinary pace' (as a *Wisden* reporter said of his 1949 bowling) who was unable to swing the ball properly, if at all, and possessed an awkward action not in accordance with all the classic principles.

Nevertheless, no one could possibly gainsay his 96 wickets at three runs apiece and it must have been clear (to a wise coach) that he had his strong points and that they already eclipsed his weaker points.

The strongest point of the young Statham's bowling which the Lancashire authorities observed was probably his accuracy. He says: "I've always had the knack of bowling straight simply because I played so much cricket. Even as a boy, I bowled literally for hours and hours."

His attitude became — and remained — that if he kept bowling straight he was bound to 'click' sooner or later. The guiding philosophy of his whole career was, "If they miss, I hit", and this also found expression in his own advice to budding fast bowlers, that is 'to make the batsman play at every ball', whatever the conditions.

The proof of the pudding was in the high proportion of his dismissals which did not require the aid of fieldsmen — 63 per cent of his first-class victims were either bowled or lbw.

Statham does write that he developed accuracy of length and direction after he joined Lancashire, but this is a matter of degree. One cannot see him having achieved the results he did for his RAF station (especially bearing in mind the yorkers he mentions) without such attributes; one imagines that he was already noticeably accurate on arriving at Old Trafford and that he progressed to even greater proficiency.

A.A.Thomson wrote: "Statham's near perfection in length and

direction was not something to which he aspired; he achieved it naturally and without strain." And Neville Cardus said of Statham's career: "Not even Larwood equalled Statham's persistent certainty of length and direction." John Arlott for his part states that the Lancashire bowler was "probably more consistently accurate than any other bowler of his pace in cricket history." [1]

As for the players' opinions, one can take two tributes to Statham's accuracy from his captain and from his bowling partner with reference to a successful tour of Australia. Hutton wrote that Statham's fast bowling there was "possibly the most consistently accurate since the days of Harold Larwood." And Tyson wrote: "I owed much to desperation injected into the batsmen's methods by Statham's relentless pursuit."

The second factor which was likely to have impressed the Lancashire authorities was Statham's ability to make the ball deviate on pitching. The stock type of ball which brought him reward, season after season, pitched just outside or on the line of the off stump and cut inwards. Of course, pitching the ball just outside the off stump would have precluded any lbw dismissal in, say, Larwood's heyday (ie before the 1935 law was introduced).

Statham says that even if he tried to bowl such a 'break-back' or 'nip-backer', the ball might still go straight on, but at least he was happy that the batsman could not possibly tell.

Far fewer of his deliveries moved away from the right-handed batsman on pitching, but on a responsive surface there were enough such balls to sow seeds of doubt in the batsman's mind.

How did Statham make the ball cut in to the right-hand batsman so often? By gripping it "with both fore and second finger on the left-hand side of the seam," recalls Tyson. Or "by body-swing, with the right arm sweeping across the ball's direction at the last split-second of release," wrote Neville Cardus, who added: "To describe him as a 'seamer' is libellous. He could bring the ball back viciously — and the press-box would tell us that he 'did it off the seam', which is a phrase that is meaningless; moreover, it is a phrase which would have us believe that a bowler can, while achieving rare velocity of flight, drop the ball's seam exactly where he would like it to drop."

However, to add fuel to the fire, let me interject a quote of Ted

[1] Written in 1971

Dexter's on Ray Lindwall: "He was so controlled, despite his pace, that he would take a new ball and ask you what bit of shine you wanted removed with his first ball. He would move it round in his hand and produce it grazed in the nominated place after pitching just once."

Cardus continues by saying that he has been told "by more than one batsman — in two hemispheres — that Statham has clean bowled them, middle or leg stump, by balls pitching outside the off — and during flight tending to swing *away* to the slips."

So now one has Statham's undisputed early strong points: his accuracy of length and direction and his ability to, so to say, 'seam' the ball off the pitch. As for his speed at this stage, opinions varied; but it was gradually increasing.

To these strong points, one must add his stamina. He was an athlete of suppleness and wiry muscle. Remember he was athletic enough to be offered a soccer trial by a First Division club; his fleetness of foot also showed in the cricket field, where furthermore, his throw from the boundary to the wicketkeeper was, in the batsman's eyes, lethal.

His philosophy on fitness was that he kept fit for bowling by bowling, a philosophy akin to that of, for example, Fred Trueman. Where special training was necessary, such as on the ship to an overseas tour, he was, unlike, say, Tyson, out of his element. This is not surprising when one considers that, owing to his suppleness, it was normal for Statham to be able to bowl his first ball of the day genuinely fast; he did not need to warm up.

Trevor Bailey regards him as an ideal net bowler, for the double reason that he was reliably accurate (and therefore safe to face in the nets) and tirelessly enthusiastic. Bailey states that Statham's ability to bowl, in effect, as the batsman ordered in the nets was of great help to him.

Indeed, Bailey points out that on the field, captains easily tended to overbowl Statham because of the very combination of his stamina and his willingness. To Neville Cardus, Statham's bowling in one Test in particular "recalled the period in which fast bowlers were expected in dry weather to bowl nearly all day," although to Bailey, that same spell meant "it was a year before Brian was quite himself again."

There is no other word than philosophical for Statham's own

attitude to his long spells of bowling. His patience and steadiness, his calm equability of temper, were renowned. He wrote in *Instructions to Young Cricketers*: "You've got to be tough to be a bowler. You must learn that there are days when you will have none for plenty. Only by accepting the fact that the ball cannot always master the bat will a bowler reach the heights."

And of bowling under Len Hutton in Australia: "Such was his devotion to the cause of quick bowling, that there were times when he outrageously over-bowled both Frank Tyson and me. I state that as an unemotional fact. I am not complaining. As I said before, I chose to be a fast bowler, and I chose to be a professional. If my captain wants to bowl me until I disappear through a hole in the ground, that's up to him. I'll keep going as long as I can."

Statham was never overweight, his normal weight being 12st 4lb, and if, as he did, he lost some 11lb between the beginning and end of a typical English season, of 760 overs on average, it was hardly a surplus 11lb.

Statham says that this 'fighting weight' contributed to his enjoying an, on the whole, injury-free career, although there were regular — and inevitable — minor injuries.

He learned the necessity to look after — or as he says "bowl a little for" — himself early in his career, when he was flown out from the desks and armchairs of his English winter straight into the tropical heat of Australia in January 1951, in order to reinforce the MCC team. This was for him a case of sink or swim.

When playing in a heatwave of 105°F he had difficulties in breathing during his run-up and he had to discover, almost overnight, how to pace himself, conserve his energy, and (as he says) "bowl full out with the minimum of effort."

What he thus learned during that early tour helped him throughout his career to try to remain fresh enough to respond to his captains' likely demands. Thus the stamina he attained was partly natural and partly cultivated by experience.

A further strong point of Statham's bowling was his run up to the wicket. Its smoothness helped to earn him the nickname of the 'Greyhound'. From the very start of his career he found the run-up which suited him best and he says he never varied it. He was, he adds, 'very deliberate' about placing the marker 13 and a half steps from the wicket throughout his career. Then he would take three extra strides, or five if he was bowling particularly fluently.

Furthermore he states, "I have always made a fetish of putting my foot down right by the side of the marker," adding "I estimate[2] 50 per cent of our bowlers straddle the marker. It is impossible to bowl well doing this. Even being six inches out can make all the difference." This attitude is reminiscent of Maurice Tate's.

So perhaps Statham was not only a natural bowler, but also one who had an infinite capacity for taking pains.

Finally, one cannot survey a fast bowler's attributes without mention of the bouncer. Certainly Statham possessed one: Bailey calls it 'nasty', Tyson calls it a 'strangulation effort' which came in to the batsman. But he used it so rarely that Trueman asserts that if Statham had a fault it was his lack of aggression. The latter's character, indeed, was not fiery but imperturbable, a word repeatedly applied to him by players and writers alike. Bailey claims that Statham did not make enough use of the bouncer, adding by way of explanation that Statham "liked people, even opposing batsmen." Tyson, however, did not find Statham quite that philanthropic!

It seems that Statham neither chose nor needed to bowl with intimidation, particularly in English 'seaming' conditions. He instinctively — for he knew it was what he was best at — bowled to hit the stumps; and if the batsman put his pads in the way, Statham could still confidently expect to dismiss him. And he did dismiss many of the great batsmen of various countries by putting this instinct into practice. Moreover, that success began early in his first-class career.

So the picture of Statham becomes that of a rare fast bowler: of a pacific one who did not rely on softening up the batsman. Another such bowler was Ted McDonald, but Neville Cardus claims to have seen him do something which he never saw Statham do — let fly a fusillade of bouncers which wasted fuel like a car backfiring.

This is not to say that the aggression of such bowlers as Trueman and Lillee, for example, was wasted, but that Statham was as true to his own strengths as any bowler one can name.

[2] In 1969

The Way to the Top

IT was Brian Statham's 20th birthday, Saturday, 17 June 1950, when he made his first-class debut. Nigel Howard, then the only amateur in the team, captained this Lancashire side against Kent at Old Trafford: Washbrook, Ikin, Geoff Edrich, Grieves, Wharton, Malcolm Hilton, Tattersall, Barlow (the wicketkeeper), Bob Berry and Statham.

Washbrook was an England regular and altogether over half the team were knocking at the England door. There is no doubt that Lancashire depended for their attack at this time on the spin trio of Berry, Hilton (both orthodox left-arm) and Tattersall.

Between them these three took well over 300 wickets for the county in 1950, helped by the spinners' pitches found at Old Trafford. The pitches were left short of water and of rolling in an effort to deal bowlers a stronger hand than in 1949. But with hot weather crumbling the turf, Old Trafford gained a quick notoriety amongst batsmen in early June.

Some ten days before Statham's debut, the following remarkable bowling took place at Old Trafford within the space of four days (three of which were playing days): the West Indian tourist and left-arm spinner, Alf Valentine, took 8 for 26 and 5 for 41 against Lancashire and then 8 for 104 in England's first innings during his debut Test.

So it was small wonder that Lancashire could afford — even though they were going for the Championship — an opening attack against Kent which comprised a 20-year-old debutant and a batsman-turned-bowler, who at that time collected under ten wickets per season: Statham and Wharton.

Lancashire won the toss and made 271, of which Washbrook scored 72. Then, late on the Saturday, Statham bowled for Lancashire for the first time — to Arthur Fagg (who was to make 2,000 runs that season) and with Washbrook's advice not to bowl to Fagg's strength (the hook) ringing in his ears.

In an over and a half Statham gave away only a couple of runs, which encouraged him, but then he bowled his worst and shortest ball that innings and Fagg mis-hooked it off the splice to forward short leg, who took the catch. Statham — and maybe Washbrook — had reason to be pleased with his speed, if not his length.

He completed his spell of 5-1-13-1 and then the spin trio dismissed Kent twice on a rain-affected pitch by Monday afternoon, needing the help only of Statham's bowling of opener Mayes with a fine outswinger at the start of the follow-on.

Thus Lancashire won by an innings and of the debutant, the *Manchester Guardian* reported: 'He achieves an excellent pace off the pitch from his medium-fast pace through the air, lifts the ball nicely from a length and generally bowls at the stumps'.

In Statham's third county match, he found a pitch which really suited him and for which he was already longing. This was at Bath on 1 July, and a little moisture made the well-marled pitch sweat. Somerset had just achieved two successive Championship victories in their Bath Festival and their opener, Harold Gimblett, had scored 84 and 79 therein. Gimblett was selected for England later that month, although injury prevented his playing.

But Statham knew, as he bowled the first ball of the match and saw it 'fizz', that conditions were on his side. Having scored a single, Gimblett received a break-back from Statham which found the gap between the bat and pad and knocked back the middle stump. Then Statham proceeded to bowl three more batsmen and dismiss another lbw. Somerset lost these five wickets while scoring their first 11 runs and Statham had figures of 5 for 5.

The Lancashire fielders were only required to watch as the new fast bowler made full use of the conditions and attacked the stumps, in a manner which announced his ability unmistakably. He finished with an analysis of 15-6-18-5 and Lancashire went on to another innings victory.

By 18 July, the county were top of the Championship table; a week before that date, the top team had been Yorkshire. Thus when on Saturday, 5 August, the Roses match at Old Trafford began, some 26,000 spectators perhaps thought — as at least one newspaper did — that the match might well decide the Championship. Lancashire, incidentally, had not won it since 1934, whilst Yorkshire were the reigning joint-champions.

Just to add spice to Statham's first Roses match, Yorkshire elected to bat on an easy-paced pitch and the man to whom Statham was to open the bowling was no less than Len Hutton. It was altogether a dramatic setting and straightaway the cricket matched it. For the first hour, reported the *Manchester Guardian*, 'nothing that can easily be imagined could have dragged a single spectator from his seat'.

Nervous of the occasion and of the opposition, Statham ran up to deliver the first ball — and promptly fell flat on his back at the popping-crease. Gingerly, he tried again and succeeded, but his third attempt also brought a fall. There was a green patch of grass, combining with his imperfect foot action, to blame. Next he managed, to his credit, to bowl four very fast balls, Hutton taking a single off the last. Now Lowson, who reached 2,000 runs that season, had the one remaining ball of the over to face. It was the fastest and, on a length, it moved off the pitch. It knocked Lowson's off stump out before his back shot was half-completed. So Brian Statham, from his eight-ball ordeal, had emerged triumphant.

Then his partner, Malcolm Hilton, dismissed Vic Wilson for two, and Statham produced a sharp inswinger which flattened Lester's middle stump before the batsman had scored. Willie Watson soon touched what to him, as a left-hander, was an outswinger from Statham, and Edrich took a brilliant catch. Thus Statham had brought about three ducks and Yorkshire were, after 45 minutes' play, 13 for 4 wickets. The bowlers' figures at that stage were: Statham 8-2-7-3 and Hilton 7-7-0-1. The former was rested after an hour, having figures of 3 for 10 in ten overs.

Descriptions of this particular spell of Statham's refer to him as very fast by any standards, encouraged as he was by a strong breeze behind him which gave him an extra yard of pace.

But if Yorkshire were down, they were not out. Norman Yardley now played a captain's innings and although he lost Hutton, dismissed by Tattersall for 18, he was helped in a century partnership by Halliday. At 3.10pm, Statham returned with the new ball (under the 65-over rule), although he was hampered by drizzle. Half an hour later, he bowled Halliday with a break-back and next ball but one trapped Coxon lbw. Again Yorkshire bounced back. Yardley, supported by Wardle's big hitting, went on to his century and was the last out for 119 out of 226. Statham's final figures were 21-4-52-5.

This innings earned Yardley a share of the main headline —

top of the front page, no less — with Statham in the *Manchester Evening News*. A smaller headline read: 'Sensational pace bowling brought 30,000 to their feet', and in the text it said that Statham's spell was 'unparalleled in the history of these games for a boy making his debut'.

The outcome of the match was a draw but Lancashire's last-wicket pair, which included Statham, scraped the four first-innings points.

There were an even more crucial four first-innings points at stake in Lancashire's last match of the season on 26 August. Surrey, second to Lancashire, who had stayed at the top since mid-July, were the opponents at The Oval and first-innings points could well give Lancashire the Championship itself. Only if Surrey subsequently won the match would Lancashire lose those four points. Only if Surrey won this game and their one remaining match — at 12 points each win — would the title go to The Oval. Other combinations would give a tied Championship.

On the morning of the match, the table read: Lancashire 220 points from 27 (out of 28) games, and Surrey 204 points from 26 games. When Lancashire began their innings badly, losing two wickets in the second over (bowled by Surridge), they decided, if they had not done so already, to limit themselves to a battle for the first-innings points. They struggled, at under two runs per over and even then by virtue of dropped catches, to 221 all out. Would this be enough to bring Lancashire their long-awaited Championship?

Statham had half an hour's bowling at the Surrey openers in the evening, his partner being an amateur, Dickinson, who appeared occasionally. Laurie Fishlock, a veteran left-hander, who topped the Surrey averages this season as he had the previous season also, promptly played a ball from Statham hard and wide to the left of Grieves at slip, who dived to take what Statham rates as one of the best catches he saw. Early on the Monday, Surrey were 39 for 3 and Lancashire were sitting pretty.

Enter a batsman of only a few weeks' standing with Surrey. Given capable support, he scored 92 before Statham had him caught at the wicket. This was the bowler's first meeting with Peter May, who won — as indeed did Statham that same month — his county cap as Surrey grasped hold of those first-innings points.

The match drifted afterwards to a tame draw. Surrey beat Leicestershire at The Oval in their final game — Bedser taking 12 for 96 — so equalling Lancashire's points total and sharing the 1950 Championship. Statham feels that his county long rued their defensive attitude in The Oval match.

So ended Statham's first few months in county cricket. In Lancashire's Championship bowling averages, he was third with 36 wickets at 15.80 each and, indeed, in the national averages he was seventh. Tattersall, in his first full season (though he was aged 28) topped both lists with distinction.

For the winter, Statham's employer of two years earlier — the accountant — generously took him back and because he had won his county cap, Statham also qualified for a small winter wage from Lancashire. Christmas came and went and in the first week of 1951, Brian Statham received a telephone call at his office. It was from the Lancashire secretary and the message was that the player had been invited, along with Tattersall, to go to Australia to reinforce the MCC tourists, whose bowlers had suffered injuries.

Statham did not believe this 'phone call. However, he gradually persuaded himself that it was genuine when both a telegram and the Press arrived at his office. He thought that, if MCC were short of opening bowlers (Bailey, Bedser and Warr were originally taken to Australia in this category), there were other replacements more likely than himself: Les Jackson, Fred Ridgway or Derek Shackleton, for example.

However, Statham did have a better average and striking-rate in 1950 than any of these three, and he had youth and probably speed on his side, although Ridgway had bowled notably fast for the last month of the season. Jackson and Shackleton had each already been given one Test chance, but had not met with marked success.

Of course, when it came to first-class experience, Statham was a non-starter; so how did this aspect come to be discounted? The decision to ask for Statham seems to have been the work of two players in Australia, Hutton and Washbrook. In the various reports, including Statham's, of the behind-the-scenes story, Hutton figures larger than Washbrook — except in Hutton's account. Either way, a vital factor was Statham's Roses performance, witnessed by the two senior players at close quarters, and opening batsmen ought to be good judges of a fast bowler. And, after all, what experience did Statham possess when he entered upon that test against Yorkshire?

The background to this shortage of bowlers in Australia was that England, having lost the first two Tests, were tackling the third (at Sydney) when a nasty ball from Lindwall broke Bailey's right thumb. This meant that a huge burden of pace bowling, in great heat, fell on to Warr (a player fresh from University and in his debut Test), Bedser and Freddie Brown and would do so for many weeks.

Brown, just aged 40, bowled 44 overs in Australia's first innings at Sydney — and at medium pace, even though he had bowled leg-breaks throughout his first-class career until the Second Test of two weeks previously. Conditions and his schoolday memories had prompted the change, but this spell caused him to limp and, all in all, spinner Doug Wright having torn a muscle just after Bailey's mishap, the summoning of the two Lancashire bowlers was understandable.

After much ado and an eventful journey — Statham had not hitherto been further than the Isle of Man — the two players arrived at Sydney Airport, where they were met by Trevor Bailey and Walter Robins, the latter being in Australia independently of the MCC tour; and of course, by the Press, who jumped to the conclusion that, of the two unknowns, the taller (Tattersall) was presumably the fast bowler. The MCC team was in Tasmania and, whilst that was the case, the two newcomers thought only of finding some net-bowling by way of preparation. Indeed, because it was raining in Sydney, they were flown across to Melbourne to practise, meeting up a few days later, at their hotel, with the team, which was making its way from Tasmania to the South Australian outback for a country match.

The MCC party was virtually unknown to Statham: Washbrook and left-arm spinner Berry were Lancashire players, but as for the rest of the team, Statham had met them once before, if at all. He had not met the captain, Freddie Brown of Northamptonshire, or the vice-captain, Denis Compton.

On 24 January, at 102°F, Statham played his first match outside England and as well as the heat and the breathing problems mentioned earlier, the hard earth made running an ordeal for the feet. In this game, he sometimes found that by the time he reached the eighth ball of the Australian over he was 'literally gasping for breath'.

The next match was a first-class fixture, against South Australia at Adelaide, a favourite haunt of batsmen. Here it was three degrees hotter still and his unprotected elbows finished the day swollen owing to sunburn. There was so little in the pitch — or the air — for him that he realized that a bowler's length and direction in Australia had to be unwavering.

In these two matches he picked up a few economical wickets, economical from the point of view of runs, not of effort. Rarely can eight overs per innings have seemed such a long spell to him. Thus it was that he learned, as mentioned earlier, to pace himself.

On 2 February, at the same ground, the Fourth Test started. Understandably enough, Statham's role was that of spectator. Bedser and Warr opened the bowling, Wright was fit again, and Tattersall made his Test debut. This was the first Test match Statham had ever watched and he noted, in particular, the bowling techniques of Lindwall and Miller. In the end, England lost rather badly but it was more their batting than their bowling which failed. England were now four Tests to nil down.

For the following game, against Victoria, Trevor Bailey returned with his hand still bandaged. Although he did not succeed as a bowler, he scored a century and was selected for the final Test. In the state match, Statham had the strange experience, for him, of opening the MCC batting at the vast Melbourne ground (he scored 16) as the game petered out into a draw. However, he does not reveal in his account that the Victoria wicketkeeper opened the bowling!

He again sat out the Fifth Test, also at Melbourne, and this time witnessed match-winning bowling by Bedser (10 for 105 in the match) and Brown, as well as Reg Simpson's 156 not out which included 64 during a last-wicket stand with Tattersall, who made ten. This was England's first defeat of Australia since The Oval Test of 1938 and there was great rejoicing.

Now it was time for the New Zealand leg of the tour, and the prospect of much pleasanter weather for bowling. Indeed, Statham soon found himself in Dunedin (in the far south) where there were clouds, wind, bad light and a rain-damaged pitch. It was the Lancashire players who were most at home. Washbrook scored 147,

Tattersall took 6 for 29 in Otago's first innings, and in their second, Statham took 4 for 17. His victims included Bert Sutcliffe, bowled by the first ball of the second innings.

This was a feather in Statham's cap because in 1949, Sutcliffe had enjoyed a wonderful season in England (with 2,627 runs, only Hutton and John Langridge scoring more), and in the 1949-50 season, at the same Dunedin ground, he had celebrated the New Year with an innings of 355. On a smaller scale, in the first innings of this particular MCC match, he had contributed half of Otago's sad 83 all out.

On 17 March at Christchurch, the first of the two New Zealand Tests began and only David Sheppard was left out of the team which had won the last Test against Australia. Bailey moved up the order to replace him. Thus, there was room and a first Test cap for Statham.

Bedser and Bailey opened the bowling and Statham was first change. New Zealand batted well but the pitch was so lifeless that the match ended in the tamest of high-scoring draws. Sutcliffe made 116 in an innings which *Wisden* called 'at least the equal of any played against England on the tour', before Statham bowled him again — his first Test wicket. His analysis was 24-6-47-1.

Statham was not selected for the Second Test, which England, who recalled Sheppard and still had five bowlers, won by six wickets with no time to spare.

As the team made its way back to England via the United States, Statham was happy, regardless of his limited success, to have had such an opportunity at the age of 20. It was an investment. He was pleased to have been chosen because it meant, as he says, that he "had caught the eye of people who matter in the game. That was a good augury for the future."

He knew that what he had learnt was already standing him in good stead when, only two weeks after landing at London Airport, he began preparing with Lancashire for the 1951 season.

Catching up on Experience

ON 5 May, Lancashire were back at The Oval, where they had ended the 1950 season in disappointment. At least they obtained first-innings points this time, helped by Statham's spell of 9-2-18-4 against the tail-enders, on the last morning of a rain-affected but closely-fought draw.

In another drawn match, Yorkshire took first-innings points at Old Trafford in mid-May, despite Statham bowling four men. And he had Hutton lbw in the second innings. Then came yet another chance to tackle Surrey, this time at Old Trafford. When the visitors began their first-innings reply, they found Statham producing, from the Warwick Road end, some of the fastest bowling to be seen in county cricket at that time. The two opening batsmen were dismissed by, respectively, a late, dipping yorker and a fine catch at the wicket, each for single figures. Then Statham had the Surrey captain lbw for 3 and in his second spell dismissed the only two real run-makers, one of whom was Alec Bedser who lost his off stump. Statham finished with figures of 20.3-4-33-5 in Surrey's 114 all out.

Surrey then followed-on and their two openers suffered the same fate as Bedser had — and for three runs between them. Statham also bowled Constable to make Surrey 34 for 3 and, as Lancashire were set only 39 to win, he finished with figures of 20-8-29-4.

On 26 May, Statham made his first appearance at Lord's where Lancashire batted first against Middlesex to make 309, although the innings ended ignominiously from Lancashire's viewpoint.

Statham, having gone in at number-eight, hit the ball for what he thought was a safe single and ran for the bowler's end. As he slid his bat past the crease, the wicket was broken, the fielders appealed and the umpire's finger went up. Statham thought he was in and says he must have given umpire Alec Skelding 'a queer look' because Skelding called him back. Statham says he was told: "Listen, son, don't you ever look at me like that again. We umpires are not infallible. We're human beings. That means we can all make mistakes. But don't let me ever catch you questioning any of my decisions." Thus Statham says he learned to respect umpires very early in his career. Then, after the run-out, Lancashire suffered a hat-trick at the hands of left-arm spinner Jack Young.

Statham, of course, was in an unequal contest with a character like Skelding. Once, also at Lord's, the veteran umpire thought that a fast bowler was making too much fuss in the placing of sawdust on a damp ground. At last, after much delay, the bowler was ready for action. Skelding dramatically stopped him half-way through his run-up, walked solemnly to the farthest mound of sawdust, picked up a pinch of it between finger and thumb, walked back to the stumps and deposited it to form his own mock foothold. Then he seriously announced: "Play!"

Notwithstanding the peremptory end to their respective innings, Statham and Lancashire were soon back in charge of the match. Middlesex were dismissed cheaply, the last few wickets going to Statham, whose analysis was 10.3-3-14-4, including the bowling of W.J.Edrich for 61, over half of his team's total. Like Surrey, Middlesex followed-on and could only set Lancashire a trifling target.

Even this, though, could not prevent Warwickshire from going top of the table on 1 June and there they stayed for the rest of the season.

The South Africans visited England this summer and although Bedser and Bailey opened the bowling at Nottingham, where the Springboks won, Statham was selected to play in the Second Test at Lord's, beginning on 21 June. He was particularly pleased because, compared to the occasion of his first Test cap, there were a lot more players available for selection.

This Test was a triumph for his colleague Tattersall, who, with almost medium-pace off-spin and a predatory leg-trap, took 12 for 101 as England levelled the series. Statham and Bedser were not required a great deal, although the former did end South Africa's largest partnership by removing Cheetham's middle stump. Statham, along with the rest of the players, was honoured by being introduced to Princess Elizabeth during the tea interval on the Friday, by which time South Africa were already following-on.

At the end of June, Lancashire won at Tunbridge Wells, Statham bagging nine victims. These included Fagg and Cowdrey (aged 18, but already outstanding) twice each and for first-innings ducks.

Statham kept his place for the Third Test, this time on his home ground. Again an England bowler took 12 wickets in the match — this time it was Bedser — and again Statham was required to bowl only 24 overs in total. He did, however, send opening batsman Waite's off stump flying with his third ball in the second innings.

England's second innings, when they needed 139 to win, was an interesting one. After a delay for rain late on the fourth day, England had to bat for the last hour on a pitch which, never easy, was now at its most difficult. In the first innings, Hutton had been hit four times in one over by lifting balls, and it was the lift in the pitch which had brought Bedser many of his victims.

Now, however, South Africa's tall, fair, 22-year-old fast bowler, Cuan McCarthy, became carried away by the viciousness of the pitch. He bowled short continually. *Wisden,* in two places, and Statham, also, stated that if McCarthy had threatened the stumps more and made the batsmen play more, South Africa could have made serious inroads into the England batting in that hour.

As it was, Ikin was hit so often that Statham descriptively says "even his bruises had bruises." But England lost no wicket that evening and went on next day to an easy victory on a quietened turf. To Statham, McCarthy had committed the cardinal sin.

Returning to the Lancashire team, Statham proceeded to take five wickets in an innings in three successive games at Old Trafford: 5 for 39 against Leicestershire, 5 for 20 against Derbyshire and 5 for 52 against Northants. On the first two occasions, he may have been galvanized by not being given the new ball, a rare event caused by conditions favouring such bowlers as spinner Malcolm Hilton.

During this successful time, he also represented the Players against the Gentlemen at Lord's and enjoyed himself as his side, led by Compton, won a fine contest by 21 runs with three minutes to spare.

As for the last two Tests against South Africa, the partners selected for Bedser were Bailey and Shackleton respectively, so Statham had to be content with two Test caps that summer.

Strangely, in August he played nine games for Lancashire but never took more than three wickets in an innings, having a total haul of 13. At the end of the season, though, with Lancashire finishing third — although a long way behind Warwickshire and Yorkshire — he topped the Lancashire Championship averages with 90 wickets at 14.65 each. Nationally, he was third in the averages in this his first full season, behind notably the versatile Appleyard, who took his 200th wicket (no less) with the last ball of what was also his first full season.

Statham put his feet up for a fortnight and then boarded the ship to Bombay for the MCC tour of India and Pakistan. He and Tattersall had accepted the chance of this always difficult tour, but no one else of the 1950-51 MCC team had done so.

The Indian tour normally needs many adjustments for the Englishman: to climate, diet, pitches and, especially in those days, accommodation, and the running of the game itself. To the team's fastest bowler, who did not like curry, or rice, or mutton, it was bound to be demanding; to him, 'any other tour is child's play' — but he recommends the trip for experience.

The players were showered with flowers on their arrival at Bombay. By 5 October, they were out on the field. Three MCC batsmen had to give their wickets away because they had to escape from the heat in the middle; and later, in Ceylon, wicketkeeper Brennan was taken to hospital with sunstroke. Generally, the fast bowlers (Statham, Ridgway and Shackleton) could not bowl full pace for more than three overs; and the humidity, which was worse than in Australia, led to the lightest of cricket clothing being soaked with sweat in no time at all.

In the second match, on coir matting, Statham tripped and realized that pointed studs were not suited to the surface, and that he was better off with crêpe rubber soles.

The First Test took place at New Delhi on 2 November and Statham briefly dislocated an elbow, although he says that this did not affect his bowling. England were in dire straits during this match but were saved by Allan Watkins, supported by Donald Carr, who was vice-captain to Nigel Howard of Lancashire.

Then the tourists ventured into newly-formed Pakistan, not at that time an official Test-playing country. On the mat at Karachi, Fazal Mahmood, bowling leg-cutters and giving hints of future fame, took 6 for 40, whilst Statham bowled at his fastest for figures of 16-7-32-4. Hanif Mohammad, aged 16 but looking more like a 12-year-old to the England fast bowlers, who (only at first) took it easy with him, made 64 by virtue of brilliant defensive technique, in four hours.

Pakistan won by four wickets and thus helped themselves into the Imperial Cricket Conference. But the umpires had played a part — no Pakistan batsman was given out leg-before, whereas Howard was, twice. Tattersall, one of the fairest appealers Statham knew, appealed 30 times (according to Statham), or at least the England bowlers between them did (according to *Wisden*). The Pakistanis used their pads fearlessly. MCC were not surprised when Pakistan, following this victory, were admitted to the ICC in July 1952.

The MCC team returned, after the visit to Pakistan, to Bombay for the Second Test, which was notable for Hazare following his 164 not out in the First Test with 155 before he was run out. However, Statham's partner, Ridgway, produced a bouncer for Hazare near the end of his innings (although Statham says the pitch was so tame that a dangerous bouncer was impossible) which the batsman mis-hooked, and it cut his forehead. This may have contributed to Hazare's failure in the rest of the series. From the English viewpoint, this drawn Test belonged to Graveney.

The next match was at nearby Poona, where Statham found himself sharing the third man boundary with a monkey. But not for long, for he ran away from its grabbing arms and the monkey returned to the crowd and watched the rest of the day's play from the top of a marquee! The match finished on 23 December, but the team managed to reach Calcutta at the other side of India in time for Christmas Day. This was spent at the European-style Bally Gunge Cricket Club.

Starting on Boxing Day, MCC played Bengal at Calcutta and Statham watched as Ridgway and Shackleton, in the second innings, took advantage of the only pace-bowler's pitch that MCC met in India or Pakistan. The Third Test was a laborious draw on a pitch which, although also in Calcutta, was dead, but the fourth game, at Kanpur, was an easy win for England.

The final Test at Madras was India's first-ever Test victory, by courtesy of all-rounder Vinoo Mankad, who had 12 for 108 in the match with left-arm spin. During the first day, the death of King George VI was announced. The rest day was brought forward to the next day, and the joy of victory for India at the end was restrained.

A few games in Ceylon completed the tour. The first was against a Commonwealth XI, captained by the Sinhalese F.C. de Saram and including Keith Miller. It seems that MCC hoped for a gentle game at this stage but that de Saram told Miller to bowl bouncers on what was the fastest pitch MCC had seen for perhaps years. Moreover, Statham was not playing. The tourists were badly defeated and the rather unnecessary aggression was a source of annoyance. But the next match was against an all-Sinhalese side, also at Colombo. MCC, with their tails up for revenge, had Ceylon 7 for 3 and then 58 all out in their first innings, thanks to Statham and Ridgway; the former bowled de Saram for a single and finished with 11-7-9-4. An innings victory followed.

The ship, the *Chusan,* left for England in early March, so after a demanding five months the team was due for a relaxing voyage. In the records, Statham had 40 wickets at 20 runs each, but there was, as there was for all the players, a wealth of experience behind such bare statistics. Although Statham feels sure it is "the hardest tour of all," he equally feels it is of benefit to a player to visit the sub-continent early in his career.

On the Test Fringe

THE season which was imminent, 1952, was disappointing for Brian Statham as far as Test matches were concerned and, following the MCC tour, harder labour than usual as far as Lancashire matches were concerned. His reward, however, was a hundred wickets in a season for the first time.

The Indians were again the Test opposition and Statham, with Ridgway, had been looking forward to bowling to them with the advantage of more responsive pitches. However, they were both frustrated in this regard, neither of them being picked for any of the four Tests.

England had a marvellously successful opening attack that summer — Bedser and the debutant Fred Trueman. This is not the place to describe Trueman's beginnings in first-class cricket. Suffice it to say that, his birth-date being within a year of Statham's, he played for Yorkshire before Statham's debut for Lancashire, although Statham was the first to become a Test player.

Trueman, like his Lancashire counterpart, was called up for National Service with the RAF, but in Trueman's case he was already a first-class cricketer at the time. Indeed, the RAF's permission was required for him to play in his debut Test series against India.

I will not go into the details of the 1952 Tests. It has already been mentioned that Bedser and Trueman were successful and from that, one can deduce that Statham was not required. Trueman took 29 wickets, which no England bowler has yet beaten in a series against India, and Bedser took 20.

So with the England bowling in other capable hands, Statham's work in the summer of 1952 was for his county. Despite the 1951-2 tour of India, which took more out of Statham (and Hilton and Tattersall) than he (or they) imagined, he took 100 Championship wickets at 17.99.

Statham felt that, partly through staleness, the bowling of all three had lost some 'snap' and Tattersall and Hilton had lost some of their capacity to spin the ball. Furthermore, he and Tattersall had to do more bowling than they really cared for, because there were few reserves of the right calibre, and at the end of the season the pair had been bowling for 20 consecutive months. Nor was there yet a regularly successful opening partner for Statham, so, all in all, Lancashire did well to finish third again in the table and their leading bowlers, in particular, showed great stamina.

Statham's 100 wickets were gathered gradually throughout the 1952 season without the aid of outstanding analyses, but in June, during a rain-spoilt draw at Old Trafford, he again, as he had done in his very first triumph, gave Somerset a hard time. After Washbrook had made 211 not out, Somerset reached 30 without loss, then Statham bowled Gimblett. He also bowled the next two men for ducks and Somerset were 30 for 3. Later in the same innings, with the new ball, he bowled two more players and finished with five, all bowled, for 32.

In July, Statham achieved a landmark with the bat — his first 50. In fact, it was 54 not out against Middlesex at Old Trafford during an unbroken stand of 149 for the eighth wicket with Grieves. Statham must have rued the declaration which followed because the Lancashire record (dating from 1900) for the eighth wicket was only one more run. (In 1979 it was raised to 158).

In the last home game of the season, against Northants, Statham produced his best spell of the summer. After the teams had matched each other with large first-innings totals over the first two days, a draw seemed likely.

At five for no wicket in the Northamptonshire second innings, Broderick drove the ball back past Statham and it hit the stumps directly with Brookes backing up too far — not out. However, Statham quickly picked up the ball and plucked out a stump — Brookes run out 2. The bowler — it seems he was in a particularly competitive mood — then tested Broderick with a bouncer or two and followed up with a yorker which uprooted his leg stump. Oldfield, a former Lancashire batsman, was lbw first ball to Statham, but there was no hat-trick: Northants 13 for 3.

Statham was at his fastest and at 23, Barrick was caught in the gully and Freddie Brown lost his off stump first ball. Again Statham missed a hat-trick but he had figures of 4 for 14 when he was rested after an hour. Eventually, Lancashire made 176 to win in 110 minutes, thanks to Geoff Edrich and two runs (including an overthrow) off the last ball of the match.

Still, Lancashire had no chance of keeping up with Surrey — even though they had in July beaten (by an innings) an Oval side depleted by Test calls. Surrey led the table from mid-June onwards and won 20 of their 28 games. It was Surridge's first season of captaincy and Surrey's remarkable spell of pre-eminence had begun.

Statham spent the winter of 1952-3 (there was no MCC tour) back at the accountants who had been so generous with his employment. It was a well-earned rest from cricket.

In the summer of 1953, the Australians visited England but as regards the Test matches, Statham had another disappointing season, playing in only one. However, he was twice 12th man. It was a period when England, encouraged by the all-round capacity of Bailey and Brown, decided to rely on only three specialist bowlers, so bowling places were at a premium in any case — except for the last and victorious Test at The Oval, where Bedser, Trueman, Laker and Lock all played important parts in winning back the Ashes.

By that stage, Trueman was preferred to Statham, partly because the former was among the wickets at the time (although he only played ten games for Yorkshire in 1953 owing to RAF service) and was more of a fearsome prospect to the Australians; and partly because Statham was perhaps a little jaded by August — Len Hutton mentions this — especially compared to Trueman. As for Bedser, he still maintained his peak — 39 wickets, beating Tate's record for an Ashes series.

Statham's only Test was at Lord's. He had been 12th man for the First Test but, following some impressive bowling for Lancashire, he made the England team for Lord's, often, as the selectors knew, a pace-bowler's pitch anyway. Incidentally, John Arlott regards Statham in 1953 as of true pace but not yet full speed. However, it turned out to be a pitch for batsmen and Statham's main attribute was economy, although he did break the Australian second-innings opening partnership: Hassett caught Evans bowled Statham 3. He also kept Miller, who scored a century, on his toes, by means of a bouncer which hit him in the chest and made him drop his bat and do a jig. The crowd, need one say, were on Statham's side. Statham says that Miller never retaliated at him, which one feels is fair. Statham also contributed a fine backwards-tumbling catch which Morris had skied to mid wicket off Compton. But the pattern of England's attack during the first four Tests was emphasized on the Monday afternoon when the new ball was given to Bedser and Bailey. This was the match which is almost synonymous with the long stand by which Watson and Bailey saved the game for England.

Statham had a leg strain at the time of the Manchester Test, which led to Trueman being 12th man. At Leeds, Statham was 12th man again and, finally, at The Oval, Trueman won his first cap against Australia in the same series in which Statham had done so.

So much for the Test Match scene. Let us now return to the start of the 1953 season to examine some of Statham's performances with Lancashire.

It was a wet summer but this did not stop him from obtaining 101 first-class wickets, of which 87 at under 15 runs each put him at the top of the Lancashire Championship averages.

In May, during the Test trial, for which he was not selected, he played for Lancashire against the Australians and felt that he bowled well, although his figures were not outstanding.

On 20 June, just before the Lord's Test, came the county match against Leicestershire, for whom 1953 was their best season: they finished equal third with Lancashire, having once led the table for the first time in their history. The Leicester pitch seemed easy, but when the home team batted, Statham, helped by a strong breeze, not only obtained good figures but also deserved better.

He began the match by having batsmen numbers two and three caught for two runs between them, but then Palmer and Lester put up a near-century stand. According to the *Manchester Guardian*, this stand would never have occurred if Statham had insisted on his attacking field of three slips, a gully and three short legs being retained during the whole of his opening spell. As it was, a snick for four had driven some of these fielders back towards the boundary, but Palmer edged his first ball over the exact spot where third slip had been at the start — and it went for four anyway! The same newspaper report doubts whether an Australian captain would have been so generous with field-settings.

The fielders were brought up again but it was too late. Towards the end of an innings of only 165, Statham bowled three other batsmen, finishing with 5 for 57. Lancashire gained a useful lead and Statham had 4 for 43 of Leicester's second innings 165 for 7 when rain washed out the last day, probably to Leicestershire's relief.

Following Statham's appearance in the Lord's Test, there came the Hampshire match at Old Trafford. Hampshire batted first on a pitch described as favouring batsmen and, indeed, as perfect. The visitors reached 271 for 2 before Statham (0 for 38 until then) bowled Harrison and Eagar for 3 and 0 and Tattersall ended Rogers' dominating innings of no less than 156. The score was now 271 for 5.

Overnight, Hampshire were 318 for 5 and were 330 for 6 when Statham took the third new ball. By means of pace and swing, he removed Rayment's leg stump, Dare's middle stump, had Shackleton caught at the wicket and yorked Prouton. This was a spell of 4 for 6 and gave him figures (once 0 for 38) of 6 for 49, which were his best-ever to that date, beating the 5 for 18 at Bath in his first triumph.

Washbrook and Ikin then proceeded to show that the pitch was blameless but, unfortunately, only a few hundred people saw this Monday's play, partly because of slow scoring by both teams. However, two sporting declarations led to an exciting win for Lancashire on the last day with five minutes to spare.

Another dramatic match for Statham, and for Lancashire, was at Trent Bridge on 5 August. Nottinghamshire batted first and Statham had both openers missed at slip before a run was scored. Simpson went on to 78 and Clay to 108. Lancashire had to concede the lead in a high-scoring first innings — but then Statham struck.

It was the last day, the pitch was wearing, and the spinners were probably licking their fingers. But Statham was retained at one end and understandably so. In his first three overs, as in the first innings, he was hostile but unlucky. Then Tattersall dismissed Clay for a single: 16 for 1, Simpson 15 not out. In Statham's fourth over, he knocked Simpson's off stump out and left the middle one leaning on the leg stump. Two balls later he had Hardstaff caught at the wicket for a duck: 16 for 3.

Next, he had Poole caught by Edrich and Stocks caught at short leg off a bouncer. He retired after just over an hour with figures of 10-5-12-4, and he had transformed the game. No matter that the tail changed his figures to 4 for 26 because, with Tattersall and Berry playing their part, Nottinghamshire were all out for 96 and Lancashire won comfortably.

The selectors met the next day to pick the team for the Test at The Oval (a six-day match to decide the Ashes), but Trueman was thought to be a better bet than Statham, as already mentioned.

Even before this final Test, a nucleus of ten players had been announced for the MCC tour to the West Indies that coming winter, and this had included Trueman but not Statham. On the Monday of the Test, five more players were added to this nucleus and these included Statham. He celebrated against Glamorgan at Swansea by taking 5 for 14.

His Test Place Assured

ALEC Bedser had previously announced himself unavailable, so the four opening bowlers for the tour were Statham, Trueman, Bailey and Middlesex's Alan Moss. The last-named had less experience of first-class cricket than the first two, so this attack faced a difficult task in a land new to all of them and on pitches renowned for being hard and true. And in a tropical sun, fast bowlers more than any other type of player are humbled by the heat.

The team flew to Bermuda on 14 December, which meant that the first match was some ten weeks later in the year than the equivalent match of the tour to India and Pakistan. Indeed, the schedule included ten first-class matches in the West Indies compared to 27 on the earlier tour (each figure halved in Statham's own case). In this respect, then, Statham could regard himself as a seasoned tourist.

Incidentally, this 1953-4 tour was the first full-strength (Bedser excepted) MCC visit to the Caribbean and the first one to be led by a professional captain.

The players stayed in Bermuda for Christmas Day, small groups of them being allocated to private homes in Hamilton. On Boxing Day, they flew on to Jamaica where they played three games at Kingston, culminating in the First Test. The first two games (one was at the Test ground) had boasted fast pitches, so the Test team included all four opening bowlers. However, the pitch for the Test at Sabina Park starting on 15 January proved to be considerably slower.

The West Indies were without Worrell, who was unfit. Thus, 44-year-old George Headley, who had scored a century in each innings of a Test against England in the year that Statham was born, gained another cap against long odds, to the delight of his home crowd, who had indeed sponsored his very presence.

Stollmeyer won the toss from Hutton, whose team was similar to that which had won the Ashes — amongst three changes, Bedser's place had gone to Statham. The West Indies series was to be of six-day Tests, perhaps because of the true batsmen's pitches, of which Sabina Park was a good example.

Statham bowled the first ball of the series and it flashed past Frederick's bat and off stump. Then after 20 minutes' play, Frederick, still not off the mark, mis-hooked Statham off the shoulder of the bat and gave a high catch to Graveney, running back from slip.

The ball quickly loses its gloss in Caribbean conditions and only when the new ball was taken did another wicket fall, when Stollmeyer was lbw to Statham. A slow day's play ended with the West Indies 168 for 2, Statham having been England's most successful bowler — and the fastest it seems — with 2 for 31 off 19 overs. This foundation to the West Indies innings proved good enough for them, over six days, to win the match. The crowd gave hints, nevertheless, of future trouble, first by bullying an umpire's family because he had given a local batsman out for 94 in the latter's debut Test. Statham says that Holt was plumb lbw to him, having tried to hook a ball which did not lift. And second, by repeatedly giving their own captain the 'bird' for not enforcing the follow-on.

A sad aspect of this defeat was the no-balling of Lock's faster ball, which the bowler cut out during his next match and for the rest of the tour. The call was, it seems, justified, but he was still allowed to bowl his faster ball when he returned to England. Trevor Bailey, from what is a sad tale, produces a humorous note in recalling Lock's shooting out Doug Insole in a Champion County versus The Rest match. After the stumps had been hit, Insole remained long enough to enquire of the umpire whether he had been bowled or run out. . .

With a flight via Antigua to Barbados behind them, the tourists faced the Second Test at Bridgetown starting on 29 January, by which time Statham had recovered from boils on the knee. Trueman and Moss were not selected, so Bailey opened the bowling with Statham who, indeed, tended to be saved by Hutton for the Tests as a matter of policy.

It did not take Statham long in this Test to make an impression on the West Indian opening batsmen, even though it was a magnificent batting pitch — perhaps a shower just before the match began helped him. Off his fourth ball, Holt snicked to Hutton chest-high and two-handed at third slip but the ball fell. Off his sixth ball, the same batsman snicked between Evans and first slip, but the former could not hold the ball, nor could the latter collect the ricochet.

At this stage, Statham had the benefit of an eight-man field between gully and short leg. When the score was ten, Holt pushed the ball to where mid on would have been, crossed for a single and belatedly noticed Stollmeyer, who was encouraged by the ground that Watson as a lone fielder needed to cover, rushing back up to him at the bowler's end. Watson threw there but Statham, with two batsmen for company, caught the ball and sent it down the pitch to the lonely Evans. Thus was the West Indies captain dismissed for a duck.

Worrell, fit again but out of practice, faced two balls from Statham, and the second, pitched right up to him, went from the bottom of his bat on to the stumps. When Holt was caught at first slip off Bailey, West Indies were 25 for 3 and Weekes, a hero of the First Test, was unavailable for this one owing to injury.

Despite being in this strong position, England did not take another wicket until the score was 190 and the bowlers could not stop the West Indies totalling 383. This turnabout was mainly the work of one man.

He was on his home ground; he reached his 50 in 65 minutes with 10 fours; despite a high backlift he hit Statham's fast yorker for four — off the back foot; in six and a half hours he hit 28 fours, both hooking bouncers and bruising the off side fieldsmen's hands, and gave only one chance, which slip just touched. Statham counts this innings among the best ever played against him and he never had such difficulty containing a batsman. In a nutshell: Walcott stumped Evans bowled Laker 220.

The upshot was that West Indies gained a large first-innings lead and went on to victory on the sixth afternoon, to go 2-0 ahead in the series.

Having flown to the mainland at Georgetown, England began the Third Test against a full-strength West Indies and again without playing Trueman or Moss. England proceeded to bat more than two days in making 435, of which Hutton scored 169. On the morning of the third day, West Indies were left with 50 minutes in which to face Statham and Bailey, and maybe the spinners, before lunch.

Statham bowled six overs, the others a couple of overs each; the pitch was unblemished at this stage — it was still to be docile on the sixth day. However, Statham did have a helpful breeze over his left shoulder and the atmosphere was probably humid because at lunchtime a tropical storm flooded Georgetown.

Statham's first ball was a wide — he slipped and it ended up at third slip. His second ball was a good-length outswinger which Worrell, opening in place of the injured Holt, snicked to Evans. Weekes late-cut a four in this over and then drove Bailey's first ball for four.

By his third over, Statham had reached his top speed. Stollmeyer played late at the third ball and snicked it on to his pad; he missed the fourth. The sixth ball probably swung in slightly and late. It pitched on middle and leg and Stollmeyer aimed to glance it, but it moved off the pitch to hit the top of the off stump with the batsman having played well inside it and still looking to the on side. The off stump flew ten yards back towards Evans.

Statham says that this was the best ball he ever bowled, but that it was a complete fluke and was "just something that happened." It is a classic illustration of his philosophy that "if I do not know myself what is going to happen, the batsman does not stand a cat in hell's chance of finding out."

His next and fourth over was to Walcott. In the Barbados match, Walcott had been caught early on at silly mid off, in the act of trying to rid himself of the fielder deliberately placed there. Now both Hutton and Bailey stationed themselves thereabouts.

Statham opened to Walcott with a tactical bouncer which found the batsman's gloves and annoyed him. The next ball was a tactical half-volley which was belted for four between the silly mid offs. Walcott tried, as the bowler hoped, to repeat this stroke to the next ball, but it was deliberately bowled from wide of the crease so that it slanted in at him. The ball also nipped in off the pitch and Walcott could only get an inside edge to it and he was bowled.

Thus, Statham had captured three wickets for ten runs and West Indies were 16 for 3. At lunch, after Statham had had Christiani in trouble, the respective figures were 6-2-12-3 and 31 for 3. A tropical storm, combated on the playing area by tarpaulins weighed down with railway sleepers, dominated the rest of the day.

This spell of Statham's was widely-praised. At the time

E.W.Swanton rated it the best by an England fast bowler (thus excluding Bedser) since the war — considering the fine quality of the batsmen and of the pitch. In retrospect, both Swanton and *Wisden* made it the turning-point of MCC's fortunes on the tour.

The West Indies followed-on — despite the crowd's violent reaction, when bottles were thrown on to the field, McWatt remained 'run out 54' — and although Statham only took one wicket, England won the match by nine wickets on the sixth day. Statham's victim was Worrell, whose three dismissals in the series so far had all been the work of the Lancashire bowler, who had only sent down seven balls to him. England had reduced their deficit in the rubber to one Test.

The Fourth Test began on 17 March at Port of Spain, Trinidad, the last to be played there on jute matting, which Bailey says was the most perfect pitch he ever saw and which had never produced a definite result in a Test. The match was full of centuries, but it was unfortunate for Statham in a different respect.

Although wearing the type of studs advised for use on the matting, he got them caught up after nine overs and tumbled down, pulling a chest muscle in the process. It was the worst injury of his career, requiring as it did a rest from cricket for some six weeks.

The match was duly drawn and England had to win the last Test, at Kingston again, in order to square the series. Despite pain-killing injections, bathing, massage and strapping, Statham needed only one gentle delivery at the nets to prove himself unfit.

In this final Test, Hutton lost the toss and Bailey and Trueman opened the bowling on another batsman's pitch. As events turned out, England could not have done better if Statham had played. Bailey produced his greatest Test achievement, by means of movement through the air and off the pitch. He encouraged these variations by bowling below his fastest and took 7 for 34 as the West Indies were all out for 139. A double-century from Hutton kept England on the road to victory, which was reached with nine wickets and a day to spare. England, from a position of two Tests down, had levelled the series.

Looking back on the contribution made by Statham, who topped the Test and overall tour bowling averages, Hutton said that he was England's biggest weapon, which is probably one reason why the captain saved him for the Tests. Hutton also pointed out that Statham left no doubt in the minds of anyone on the tour that he would be a key bowler in Australia the following winter. This was something Hutton had been keenly aware of for several years — the possibility of England finding a pair of bowlers to answer back the likes of Lindwall and Miller. The captain had relished Trueman's success in 1952. Now he relished Statham's success in the West Indies, which one feels represents the Lancashire player's permanent arrival as an England opening bowler.

When Statham reported to Old Trafford in April for the 1954 season, he could still notice the chest-muscle injury of mid-March, but he was able to play in Lancashire's first match beginning on 8 May. This was to be the wettest English summer since 1903 and tarpaulins and railway sleepers might have been tried with advantage!

The rain prevented Lancashire from having any play on 19 complete days, quite apart from interrupted days. This was one reason why the team slipped to tenth in the Championship. However, Statham's wickets were taken particularly economically — in the Championship at 12.27 each — and he topped the national averages (discounting two bowlers who took under 15 wickets), although he did not quite reach a hundred first-class wickets.

The Pakistanis were the visiting tourists and Statham partnered Bailey in the First Test, at Lord's. Victory went to the rain. The first three days saw no play, which involved the cancellation of the Queen's visit to Lord's on the Saturday, both teams going to Buckingham Palace instead. Statham and Tattersall had so little advance notice that they had to appear in sports jackets and flannel trousers! The Duke of Edinburgh presented Hutton with a sixpence, the toss-up not yet having taken place, with the result that the captain won choice of innings for only the fourth time in 15 Tests.

Play began at 3.45pm on the Monday, and in an academic contest, the bowlers enjoyed themselves most. Statham's figures in Pakistan's 87 all out were 13-6-18-4, all of his victims being bowled, as follows.

Replacing Laker at the Pavilion End on the final morning, Statham in his first over saw Kardar, the Pakistan captain batting at number-six, miss the first four balls before being bowled by the fifth. Statham quickly hit the off stump of two tail-enders for figures of 3 for 0 in 13 balls and then found the same target again to have 4 for 10 in the six-over spell. Pakistan had gone from 50 for 3 overnight to 87 all out, the England spinners also being in on the act. The match, of course, was still drawn.

During the next month, Statham several times took five wickets in an innings for Lancashire, played for the Players against the Gentlemen and contributed to England's innings-victory in the Second Test, when Compton made 278. The Third Test at Old Trafford was spoiled by rain but, on a personal note, it was made memorable for Statham because during it his wife, Audrey, gave birth to their first child, Terence. It was fortunate for the new parents that the Test was in Manchester and that there was only play on two days.

On 31 July, came the Roses match at Old Trafford. The pitch was described as a 'pudding' and the groundsman, Harry Williams, estimated that there had been 100 hours of rain in the preceding week. Statham and Colin Smith of Cambridge University opened the bowling and the conditions were emphasized when Statham, fielding at mid on, twice slithered in the mud before he could set off after Lowson's drives. But the bowlers did get on top. Statham opened with three maidens and had Watson caught at the wicket off a ball which left him, Close caught at gully off the bat handle, and Lester yorked middle stump. Smith having dismissed Lowson early on, Yorkshire were now 34 for 4 and Statham had figures of 3 for 13. This was news enough to make the main front-page headline of the *Manchester Evening Chronicle* — shades of the beginning of the 1950 Roses match at Old Trafford.

Also as in that match, Yorkshire staged a recovery stand involving Yardley. He — undeterred by being hit on the instep and thigh by Statham — and Wilson put on 170 before Statham had him caught. Statham dismissed Illingworth and Wardle for ducks to finish with an analysis of 29.3-11-76-6 in a total of 248. Unfortunately for Lancashire, 248 was enough for a Yorkshire victory by an innings — Wardle took 9 for 25 in Lancashire's first knock.

The Fourth Test at The Oval is famous for Pakistan's victory and Fazal Mahmood's 12 for 99. It was also Frank Tyson's first Test and he and Statham foreshadowed the pattern, if not the success, of England's opening bowling to come in Australia. The team for the Ashes series had already been announced — indeed Bailey and Bedser were omitted from the Test at The Oval in order to give some Test experience to future tourists, Tyson and Loader. It was strange that the careers of Statham and Tyson, who were both born in the same month and in the same county, who both played in the Central Lancashire League at the same time, and who both played for the Lancashire Second XI, did not cross until August 1954 at The Oval.

In 1954, Tyson earned his place for the coming Australian tour by taking 70 wickets in his first full season for Northants, mainly by sheer pace. His career had been slow getting off the ground owing to University studies, injuries, Army service — and a relationship with Lancashire CCC which had a jinx on it.

It had been four years previously that Len Hutton had first met Tyson. Hutton, always on the look-out for a new fast bowler, had faced him in a one-day Yorkshire pre-season match at Redcar, when Tyson was an undergraduate at Durham. The bowler's opening over was so fast (Hutton remembers having been taken aback by a ball which hit him on the pad before he could bring his bat down) that after the game Hutton asked Tyson for his address for future reference.

Tyson eventually found his way to Northants, through Jock Livingston, the man who had recommended Statham to Lancashire in 1949. In 1951, after a Staffordshire League exhibition match, Livingston, by then a Northants player, recommended Tyson to apply to the Midland county and that was that, subject to residential qualification.

I will mention one or two other points about the background to Tyson's arrival at Test level. In 1953, he played for his county against the Australian tourists in only his second first-class game and took two wickets in his first over. McDonald was lbw to the second ball and Hole was bowled middle stump by the fourth. It was an interesting portent and, all in all, there was just enough evidence by August 1954 to warrant Tyson's selection for Australia. Even on his first-class debut, against the Indians in 1952, he had been recognized by the surprised batsmen, the slip fielders and his Northants captain, as amongst England's fastest bowlers. The gamble was on his inexperience and inaccuracy. Perhaps Statham would turn out to be a suitable partner in these respects.

For the record, Tyson took 4 for 35 in Pakistan's first innings in The Oval Test, but now the season was finishing and in September the MCC team left Tilbury in the *SS Orsova* for Perth. The opening bowlers were Statham, Tyson, Loader, Bedser and Bailey — not Trueman.

Statham & Tyson

MCC began the tour well by winning the first two first-class games, both at Perth. Fast bowling was to the fore for two reasons. First, the pitch at Perth was the fastest Statham ever saw — Bedser and Bailey place it equally highly — and this tour as a whole boasted the fastest and bounciest pitches that Statham met in his career, with Perth top of the list. Second, MCC put the opposition in to bat in each match, which illustrated Hutton's thinking: "I wanted to impress Australians, both at Perth and far away on the other side of the continent, right away with our fast bowling strength" and further: "This determination to do everything to help the fast bowlers gain a psychological advantage over the Australians dominated all my tactics up to the First Test."

So wrote the man who had faced the brunt of Lindwall and Miller through four earlier series and who now saw the glint of a shining opportunity for revenge.

On 15 October, against Western Australia, Statham found immediate success in his first match. Helped by a breeze, he bowled batsmen numbers one and three, and with Bailey chipping in, Western Australia were 7 for 3 wickets. At that score, Statham forced the opposing captain to retire, hit on the head, but the batsman was able to return. Later in the innings, Statham dismissed four more players to finish with an analysis of 10-4-23-6, of whom five were bowled. It was his best first-class analysis to date and victory followed.

When Tyson played at Perth, he bowled fast but not accurately. However, he too succeeded in the next match when, at Adelaide, he took 5 for 62, although the South Australian openers enjoyed a century partnership.

On 5 November, Bedser, who had been a victim of shingles in the right shoulder, played his first match and by 19 November, MCC were playing at the sub-tropical venue of the First Test, Brisbane, which they reached by aeroplane. This match was drawn, a curiosity for Statham being that he dismissed and was dismissed by Wally Walmsley, once of the Central Lancashire League.

But there were other less parochial curiosities about Brisbane. The pitch for the Queensland match was very fast and green and the adjacent Test pitch was also green. Hutton studied the state match as a spectator and with McConnon injured, Appleyard unfit and Wardle not in form, he thought of including four quick bowlers in the Test team. Indeed, this is what Hutton and his co-selectors (Edrich and Evans chiefly) did decide upon and, according to both Statham and Tyson, it was this decision, rather than that of Hutton to put Australia in to bat, which was the more unfortunate.

Given such a bowling line-up, it was sensible to put Australia in. However, the fact that the pitch could not be watered immediately before the Test, owing to the Queensland match, made it easier-paced. And *Wisden* says that 12 catches were missed by England, although Tyson says they were not easy. Bedser was still suffering from the effects of shingles and Tyson from an over-long run-up; Statham's Achilles' heel in this innings was his share of the dropped chances. If one adds that Compton broke a bone in his hand on the boundary fence on the first morning, then the reader is perhaps prepared for the fact that Australia scored 601 for 8 declared and won by an innings.

Statham's analysis (in eight-ball overs) of 34-2-123-2 was not so bad as the average of the figures of Bedser, Tyson and Bailey, which is not saying a lot for anybody. Nevertheless, Statham was credited by both the English and Australian correspondents of *The Times* with top-class bowling during the first and second days.

The match against Victoria, beginning on 10 December, preceded the Second Test. Statham endows this state match with special significance, although he was not playing. This significance concerned Tyson. The latter had taken 1 for 160 at Brisbane, but luckily there was a panacea awaiting him. This had been suspected by Hutton and the Surrey coach, Alf Gover, at the Test at The Oval four months earlier. Hutton's opinion had been strengthened in the nets at Perth and in the Brisbane Test. On the latter occasion, Tyson began to see the light and for the Victoria match he took the plunge, cutting his run-up by some ten yards.

As Hutton had suspected at The Oval, and proved to his own satisfaction in the nets at Perth, Tyson's shorter run produced far greater accuracy at virtually the same speed. There was thus both a saving in the bowler's energy and an increase in the batsman's discomfort. The main reason Tyson had used his long run-up was that it gave him a flowing follow-through which, he says, took the jolt away from his braced left leg at delivery. But he had taken things too far — with a run-up of some 25 yards, he had needed 11 minutes to bowl an eight-ball over.

So, his mind jerked into action by having tried a short run in the heat of Brisbane, Tyson threw himself into the experiment, with the advantage of having, in any case, used a short run during his days in league cricket. Against Victoria, instead of 22 to 30 yards, he ran 15 yards, mainly made up of ten deliberate strides up to delivery. Statham says that Tyson often lost his long run-up anyway. The result at Melbourne was an analysis of 21-3-68-6, five of these victims, including Harvey, being bowled.

For the Second Test at Sydney, starting on 17 December, there was no justification, either in form or in the condition of the pitch, for continuing with the unbalanced attack of Brisbane. Places were found for two spinners and Bedser was the bowler who was dropped. This decision spelt the virtual end of his England career, in sad and controversial circumstances. Morris put England in to bat — the pitch had sweated — which produced the required result. The score was 111 for 9 when Statham walked out — and proceeded to contribute 14 not out in a last-wicket stand of 43 with Wardle. This stand took only 23 minutes and Statham says that the runs were by courtesy of the Australian 'keeper not being allowed to stand up to the stumps to Johnston whilst Wardle was down the pitch slogging.

When Australia replied on the first evening, Bailey opened with Statham to try to ensure that not a ball was wasted during that half-hour and he had Morris caught to vindicate that policy. Next day he partnered both Statham and Tyson.

The bowling of these three on the second afternoon was so good — conditions favoured them just the necessary amount — that *The Times* likened Australia's middle-order batsmen to players practising in front of a mirror. With the ball swinging and lifting, they relished a single to take them to the other end.

During this innings, Statham often just beat the bat or the stumps and chances were missed off him, one of them easy. But he dismissed Benaud lbw to a break-back. And he made Davidson play on. Tyson improved greatly to take 4 for 45, which included Lindwall, frightened by a bouncer into snicking to Evans (Lindwall had scored 64 not out at Brisbane). Bailey had four wickets too but, even so, Australia made 228, for a lead of 74.

May and Cowdrey were now responsible for England's useful second innings but the latter stages saw Tyson knocked out by a Lindwall bouncer, on which Tyson turned his back. After lunch and an X-ray, he was able to resume but England were 250 for 9 — a lead of 176 — when Statham joined Appleyard. The pair added 46 sensibly in 53 minutes for the last wicket, Statham scoring 25.

As *The Times* pointed out, Statham now had made 81 runs in five innings against Australia and it seemed as if the reporter was about to praise his batsmanship highly when he wrote that Statham was into position before the ball was bowled. However, the effect was spoiled by his explaining that Statham did not believe in using his feet!

Statham was able to send the ball in many directions by means of a keen eye. His own comments, quoted by Cardus, on his important batting in this match (and on his bowling) were: "When I bat and miss I'm usually out. When I bowl and they miss, well — *they* are usually out."

Australia, meanwhile, needed 223 to win and to go 2-0 up.

Statham bowled his first over as though determined to win the match on his own. Favell nearly played the first ball on. The second ball brought an lbw appeal. The fifth ball Favell snicked hard to Edrich, who touched it with both hands but it went through for two; the last ball produced a snick to the fine leg boundary. Statham's second over was an anticlimax, a reaction to the first, but his third over, the last before tea and with the score 27 for 0 in 25 minutes, saw him beat Morris, who was admittedly going for his strokes, four times in five balls and finally have him lbw pulling at the seventh.

After tea, Statham's last three overs of the spell were maidens, then Appleyard replaced him, too soon according to *The Times'* Australian correspondent. This was ironic because Statham says (objectively) that he and Tyson were regularly overbowled in this series. So much did Hutton relish their effect, that ideally, he seemed to want to bowl them through whole innings.

Tyson, in the first over after tea, dismissed Favell by sheer pace, but Burke and Harvey saw Australia slowly to 72 for 2 overnight, needing another 151.

As the fifth day began, Statham admits to having had butterflies but Tyson's second over helped. He yorked both Burke and Hole and thereby must have revolutionized the betting, and the atmosphere in the Australian dressing-room. The pitch, though never slow, was less fiery on this fifth day than on any other, but Statham and Tyson generally in this match produced more pace and lift than Lindwall. And Tyson had realized, from seeing Lindwall, the advantages of pitching the ball up, while all three England pace bowlers sensibly chose to attack the off stump. Benaud left before lunch, when the score had crept to 118 for 5, caught off Appleyard.

In his second over after lunch, Tyson produced a break-back to bowl Archer: 122 for 6, with 101 more needed. Now, the bowling was entirely in the hands of Statham, from the Noble Stand end and against the wind, and Tyson. When Davidson snicked the former's outswinger off the splice (a much-used part of the bat in this series), Evans leapt towards first slip and, in mid-air and open-mouthed with exhilaration, caught the ball two-handed: 127 for 7.

Enter Lindwall, who, of course, had the day before more than got his own back on Tyson in the exchange of bouncers. Or perhaps by now he was wondering whether he had, because the truth was that Tyson, upset but directing his energies intelligently, was doubly determined to have the last laugh by winning the match for England.

When Tyson, resisting a bouncer, bowled a full-length ball to Lindwall, the latter, to his horror, could only play it on to off stump. The score was 136 for 8. Surely England would level the series now? At 145, Statham bowled wicketkeeper Langley, breaking the off stump in the process so that when last man Bill Johnston reached the middle, he carried a replacement stump in his right hand and his bat in his left. Surely Australia were about to be humiliated?

Johnston began his joint search with Harvey for 78 runs by missing Statham's first four balls to him and surviving an lbw appeal off the next. But then Harvey took over and protected Johnston from the strike whilst playing well himself. At about a run-a-minute the pair scored nearly half the required number of runs, and then saw Statham retire after 85 minutes' bowling into the wind since lunch. His analysis was 19-6-45-3 for the innings.

Tyson was exhausted as he bowled the last over of his spell of 90 minutes with the wind, from the Hill End, but at least Johnston now had to face a full over — he faced only about nine of the 56 balls of this partnership. In the preceding few minutes Harvey had reached the 90s by means of two lofted drives to the boundary off Bailey. Thus, Hutton and his team, their lifeline reduced to 42 runs, were becoming anxious.

Tyson's tiredness was making him stray down the leg side to the left-handed Johnston, who now picked up a boundary to long leg with almost a one-handed swat that he had been employing. The crucial ball, however, was imminent. Encouraged by Statham, who was fielding nearby, Tyson now bowled a similar ball, Johnston snicked it and Evans caught it. At last, at 3.10pm, England had won the match — by 38 runs — and levelled, indeed, reversed the course of the series.

Statham and Tyson shook hands on the field, and led the England team in together. Later on, they praised each other in print: Statham says that Tyson was "at least a couple of yards faster" than himself in this match and that even viewing Tyson from third man or long leg was, at times, frightening. Tyson says of his partner: "To me it felt like having Menuhin playing second fiddle to my lead."

As for the match, Statham calls it his most tense and demanding Test. At 4pm he went to the hotel and slept for two hours, which was quite out of character. Tyson also rates this game as something special — he regards it as the best he ever played in and his performance in it (10 for 130) as the best and most enjoyable of his career.

The match was highly praised by the Press as being good for cricket. R.S.Whitington, a writer and a former Australian first-class player, found in the second afternoon's battle some of the quality of the legendary 1902 series. And in the final even contest between Harvey and Tyson, he felt he was seeing batting and bowling which had never been surpassed.

The scene now switched to Melbourne where England opened the Third Test, on a pitch producing lift, with a meagre 191. Yet 22-year-old Colin Cowdrey reached a great century.

On the second day, Australia made 188 for 8 and Statham was

England's best bowler (he had 3 for 49); Tyson was looking tired — and not because it was New Year's Day. Bowling was hard work, aggravated by great heat and by a run-up area as hard as marble. Statham fell more than once and he skated about during run-ups. Hutton, who had slipped whilst batting, helped him by changing him to the northern end. Statham took two wickets with his first ten balls from that end. His first ball moved off the pitch and Miller snicked it low towards first slip, whither Evans dived and took the catch which would not have carried to slip. In Statham's next over, Favell, who had been lucky with edges earlier, suffered the indignity of being 'ankle before wicket' — the shorn and now baked pitch was showing its vagaries.

Statham's next wicket was towards the end of the day, when he yorked Lindwall (who nearly hit Statham with a bouncer in this match). Australia were three runs behind at the close.

That weekend was Melbourne's hottest ever — the temperature was in the 90s all Saturday night and 105°F at noon on Sunday. Because it was from the north, the wind brought no relief and the atmosphere was likened to that of a pottery kiln. Shade was ineffective.

At the ground on the Monday morning, the pitch, having been open to the sunshine, was expected to be more cracked than ever, but instead it had improved and spikes bit rather than skidded. This caused a controversy over suspected watering, but be that as it may, Statham, amongst others, believes that there was no attempt to fix the result of the match, only an attempt to save the reputation of the venue.

Australia added enough to gain a lead of 40, but Statham captured the last two wickets at a cost of 11 runs so that he finished with 5 for 60 to bag five in a Test innings for the first time. This was despite again tumbling twice whilst bowling, but he had the last laugh when he sent Johnston's off stump flying. John Arlott reported that Statham was unlucky not to have an even better analysis.

England now made 279, thanks mainly to May, so that Australia needed 240 to win. They had plenty of time to get the runs, but England had had the best of the 'new' pitch and it was now being baked again.

Australia reached 75 for 2 by the end of the fourth day, thus requiring another 165 to win. Fifty thousand people arrived to see them try (making a crowd aggregate of 300,000 for the match), but the pitch was on England's side. Statham bowled three or four consecutive shooters, which Miller managed to stop, and conditions looked ideal for the spinners to follow.

But would Statham and Tyson need relieving? Play started at noon and these two met with immediate success. Helped by quicksilver behind-the-wicket fielding, Tyson, from the southern end, took three wickets in under half an hour. For one of them, what Tyson calls the fastest ball he ever bowled, led to a slip catch from Miller which was so hot it needed two men to complete it. Now half the side were out for 87.

Ten runs later Statham, having deliberately sent three successive yorkers to Hole, put a ball down of cuttable length. It moved slightly off the pitch and the batsman fell to a faint snick off the bottom edge.

Tyson dismissed Maddocks and Lindwall in three balls, so that Australia had only two wickets left and their total score was not yet 100. Less than an hour earlier, the score had been 77 for 2. It was Tyson's finest hour — and also one of England's.

Statham struck Archer on the foot with a yorker and then bowled him with a ball, which, by dint of being both a near-yorker and a creeper, shot under his bat. Finally, Evans took his third catch and, like that which had dismissed Harvey at the start of play, it was literally a match-winner.

The time was only 1.20pm, England had won by 128 runs and late arrivals were not the only people who were taken aback.

That morning, Tyson's analysis was 6.3-0-16-6 and Statham's was 6-1-19-2. In the complete innings their respective figures were 7 for 27 and 2 for 38. But Tyson has always been generous about Statham's contribution, from the moment he insisted that Statham joined him in leading the players through the pavilion gate. He later wrote: "I had taken 7 for 27, but it might easily have been Brian who returned the figures. For my part, I prefer to say that we took nine wickets between us."

In the two successive victories which had now given England a 2-1 lead in the series, Statham (12) and Tyson (19) had taken 31 of the 40 Australian wickets. And they had earned them too, by bowling nearly two-thirds of England's overs.

Statham does not complain about this amount of bowling — he believed that the decision was rightly the captain's and that his own job was to accept it. And he appreciated being rested in between Tests, which was also part of Hutton's policy.

Now Statham, having finished playing in the Test on 5 January, had nearly a fortnight without a match. So did May, Edrich and Evans. Some of the other players had a light time during the leisurely two-match visit to Tasmania.

Returning from Tasmania, the team flew via Melbourne to a two-day match (not first-class) against a South Australian Country XI at Mount Gambier. The town, just out of Victoria on the coastal route to Adelaide, was being granted (because its population had reached 10,000) its city charter, which was a cause for celebration.

As for the match itself, the honour of the MCC's visit might also have been reason for celebration, but the score hardly was:

South Australian Country XI
(Second Innings)
v MCC, 19 January 1955.

G.Fuller	b Bedser	0
H.Bennett	not out	14
K.Hanna	lbw b Bedser	2
J.Milnes	b Bedser	0
P.Eaton	b Statham	15
J.Gwynne	b Statham	0
L.Curtis	b Statham	0
M.Darling	b Statham	0
L.Beare	b Statham	0
W.Pengilley	b Statham	0
G.Gross	lbw b Bailey	14
Total		**45**

Such is the bare bones of what happened when the Country XI followed on more than 200 runs behind MCC.

January 19 was the first wet morning in Mount Gambier for weeks and the start, on this second and last day of the match, was delayed until noon. This weather aided the bowlers, and by early afternoon the local team were following-on, having lost their remaining eight first-innings wickets in the interim.

Bedser bowled the opening over of the Country XI's second innings and, indeed, he took a wicket with his first, third and eighth balls. Then play was less eventful until at 27 for 3 Statham came on to bowl, he and Appleyard replacing Bedser and Tyson.

With his third ball, Statham bowled Eaton middle stump with a shooter: 27 for 4. In his second over, he bowled Gwynne. In his third over he bowled Curtis with his first ball and later Darling. The score was now 27 for 7.

At the opposite end, Bennett hit Appleyard to the boundary. Statham followed with his fourth over, of which the first two balls bowled Beare and Pengilley respectively. Thus, Statham's analysis after 26 balls was 3.2-3-0-6. Not only that, but every victim was clean bowled.

The Times reported: 'It was great cricket and the small boys who sat on the high cypress fence about the ground could scarce forbear to bounce'.

The last batsman, Gross, prevented a hat-trick and went on to score a couple and a single off the over, so that Statham finished his spell with figures of 4-3-3-6.

Bailey replaced him and soon ended the match, which was won with only 20 minutes to spare, for all Statham's devastation.

Bennett carried his bat — but he had hardly faced a ball from Statham. Still, I should think Bennett would be a man worth asking for his opinion of Statham's bowling.

The Fourth Test at Adelaide shortly afterwards saw England, on a beautiful pitch, gain a first-innings lead of 18.

So the match and therefore the series were far from settled when Australia batted again. They reached 69 for 3 before the close of the fourth day — and, strangely, Statham, although he had suffered a couple of dropped chances, had not actually taken a wicket in either innings. This was partly owing to an injury to his left big toe.

He had previously had trouble with the nail and just before this Test the nail was removed by masseur Harold Dalton. Statham's usual padding to counteract a sore toe, however, now had little effect, so during an interval at Adelaide a hole was cut out of the leather toe-cap. This was a great relief to him, and he was ready for the eventful fifth day.

Tyson recalls that on that day he and Statham went for a run along the beach before breakfast. The morning newspapers were seen to predict that Appleyard, who had taken all three wickets for 13 the previous evening, was the danger man on the now turning pitch. Nor was there a new ball for the fast bowlers.

Yet, for that morning session of 90 minutes, Hutton bowled Statham and Tyson throughout, in a temperature always above 90°F. If Bedser was watching, he probably recalled being led off with sunstroke here on his first tour.

This time Tyson was nearly exhausted for the last quarter of an hour before lunch, but Statham encouraged him from mid off. And what reason for encouragement there was. These two bowlers had reduced Australia from 69 for 3 to 103 for 9 by lunch. The Ashes were perhaps a stone's throw away and Hutton's policy had been vindicated. Statham's morning analysis was 7-0-12-3, Tyson's was 7-1-17-3.

Statham, 5-0-26-0 overnight, found unexpected movement off the pitch on the resumption. After his third ball had yorked McDonald, his 11th, a break-back, removed Miller's leg bail. In his third over, Statham dismissed Maddocks lbw (a spell of 3 for 4), and with Benaud already fallen to Tyson, Australia were 79-7. Nor had the bowlers resorted to bouncers.

By 2.30pm, Australia were all out for 111 for the second time in successive Tests. England needed 94 and, despite Miller's efforts, they made it — winning a series in Australia for the first time since Jardine's tour of 1932-3.

The last Test was rain-spoilt. Statham ended the series with 18 wickets at 27.72, Tyson with 28 at 20.82.

March saw the team fly to New Zealand. At Wellington, Statham and Tyson were not playing, but they were given timed tests of their bowling speed. The figures showed that Statham bowled at 85mph and Tyson at 89mph, but Tyson was faster than this when flat out. Indeed, neither player removed his sweater for the trial and the conditions were wet.

At Auckland, Statham played his part in dismissing New Zealand for 26 in their second innings. This was and still is a record low total for a Test. South Africa had been all out for 30 against England in 1895-6 and in 1924, due to Lohmann's bowling on the earlier occasion and to Gilligan's and Tate's on the second.

This time Appleyard took 4 for 7 and Statham had figures of

9-3-9-3. Statham accounted for John Reid, Rabone, the Kiwis' skipper, and the last man, whose middle stump was sent flying.

During this match, Statham learned that his mother had died. But he could not have got back to England in time for the funeral and so played out this last game of the tour.

It was almost April now and everyone had earned their homeward ticket and a rest before the new season. But first there was an uncomfortable four-night aeroplane journey to London, plus days for sightseeing at places like the Hawaiian Islands, San Francisco and New York.

Statham's Test

WITHIN a matter of weeks of arriving back home, Statham was playing for Lancashire against Oxford University. The summer of 1955, although slow to warm up, was to become gloriously sunny, even if perhaps rather tame compared to Australia in January.

Swansea was the venue of Lancashire's first Championship match and Statham immediately excelled. He dismissed Wooller but, because the pitch was turning, he was taken off at 20 for 1. He was brought back at the other end, at 61 for 2, and then took 5 for 9 to push Glamorgan to 77 all out. He beat most of the batsmen by swing, and particularly by swinging yorkers, and finished with his best analysis to date of 14.3-7-17-6. The *Western Mail* reported that he 'looked what he really is — the most accurate speed-bowler in the game today'. Unfortunately, rain prevented a likely Lancashire win.

On 18 May, against Warwickshire, came Lancashire's first home game but Statham did not make the visitors welcome. Nor did the weather, for after Warwickshire had scored one without loss overnight, in reply to Lancashire's 274, rain, hail and even a snow shower prevented play until 2.30pm on the second day. The sun was drying the pitch and after tea, Statham, with the wind behind him, produced another spell of 5 for 9 as Warwickshire lost their last seven wickets for 30 in 65 minutes. This spell was 10.1 overs and the victims were all bowled or lbw.

But Lancashire collapsed and on the last day, Warwickshire needed 189 in 255 minutes. Again they could not keep Statham at bay. In his third over, the second ball kept low and bowled Horner, whilst the last ball hit Wolton's leg stump. Next, Spooner was taken at first slip so that Warwickshire were 11 for 3, of which Statham had three wickets for two runs. After an hour, Statham was rested and Gardner and H.E.Dollery, on a now dried pitch, progressed to 86 for 3 before Gardner had to be carried off, having strained his back whilst driving. Lancashire now swept the opposition aside, Greenhough dismissing two men in an over and

Statham two in two balls. Statham finished with 5 for 21 for match figures of 10 for 48.

So he had 18 wickets of the first 34 which Lancashire captured in this Championship season. Moreover, his 64.4 overs had only cost 81 runs and his wickets 4½ runs each.

Tyson and Statham joined forces again against Cheetham's South Africans for the First Test at Nottingham. England's victory owed much to Tyson for his 6 for 28 in the last innings.

On 15 June, Lancashire visited a club ground, Hinckley, to meet Leicestershire. Lancashire won an important toss and made a good start before a drying and quickly-wearing pitch caused a collapse against the spinners: 224 all out.

Leicester went in late in the day and, with the ball keeping very low, Statham, with his first and sixth balls, bowled each opener for a duck. Then he bowled Tompkin and the Australian, Vic Jackson. All this was within his first 34 balls, to make the home side 10 for 4. Smithson was missed by the wicketkeeper off his second ball from Statham, and Leicester were 12 for 4 overnight, Statham's figures being 8-4-6-4.

The next morning Statham quickly knocked back Palmer's leg stump and Munden's off stump. Thus, the first six Leicester batsmen back in the pavilion had been bowled by Statham, who had conceded only nine runs. Tattersall now dismissed three men as Leicester went from 18 for 6 to 25 for 9, and in came last man, Boshier. Here was a player who had not scored in his nine previous innings and who had his bat labelled 'Running in, please pass'! Yet he now hit Statham for ten runs and made the top score of his team's 42 all out. Statham finished with 6 for 20.

Leicester followed-on without opting for the roller. They were out even more quickly this time, although they reached a total of 81. The bowlers shared the wickets evenly and when the match ended, 16 wickets had fallen in the day by 3.10pm. Statham bowled for two hours 40 minutes, that is until 3pm, for five of those wickets.

Against Worcestershire at Old Trafford in the next match, Lancashire made 328 (Washbrook 170) and then Statham bowled opener Lister for a duck before close of play. On the Monday morning, after a rainy weekend, it was at one time nearly too misty to see the Railway Stand from the pavilion steps opposite, but play started at 1pm, despite the dismal conditions.

Statham made the ball lift awkwardly but, allowing for the recent rain, the pitch was surprisingly docile. Kenyon batted at his best, but Statham's turn soon came. He dismissed Kenyon (thanks to Ikin's brilliant two-handed overhead catch at point), Devereux, Dick Richardson and Broadbent for four runs. Then, having bowled for 65 minutes, he was rested for 50 minutes.

Only when he returned did another wicket fall, for he sent back Horton and Yarnold for figures of 7 for 34, the first occasion he had taken seven wickets in a first-class innings, let alone the first seven.

He was not to take all ten wickets, Tattersall getting in on the act, but he finished with an analysis of 27-12-43-7. All out for 136, Worcester subsequently fought back but Lancashire just had time to win.

On Thursday, 23 June, of that same week, Statham was at Lord's for the Second Test against South Africa. He probably knew that the green pitch and cloudy atmosphere which characterized this Test, should favour his bowling. In his enthusiasm, he never spared himself— and in the end, he triumphed.

May, in his first series as captain, won the toss and, faced with a difficult decision, chose to bat. The South African fast bowlers, Heine and Adcock, must have been amazed, said *The Times,* 'to find themselves moving the ball about as they could never hope to do at home'. Heine, on his debut Test, took 5 for 60 as England made 133 all out.

Statham surprised McGlew with the pace and lift of the first ball of South Africa's innings, and Evans took the catch. At the other end, Trueman was appearing in his first Test since the tour of the West Indies, replacing Tyson, who had injured his heel.

After tea, the pitch was more docile and at the close of play, South Africa had edged ahead with five wickets left, thanks to McLean. So they already had quite a chance of levelling the series.

Indeed, the next morning they did not lose a further wicket until the stroke of lunch. *The Times* thought that Statham's bowling was England's 'only saving grace'. Trueman was put off his stride by no-ball trouble caused by dragging his back foot. And several catches were dropped, notably by Bailey and Trueman in the slips in Statham's first over of the day to McLean, who cashed in aggressively.

The pitch was easing, as expected, but *The Times* thought that Statham 'bowled his heart out in as fine a spell of sustained speed and accuracy as one is likely to see this year'. Keith and McLean (again) were dropped, and *The Times* continued: 'What the Gods were giving to the batsmen with one hand they were taking from Statham with the other — no new experience for poor Statham. It is as well that he has a big heart.'

His 11.4 overs up to lunch had produced many involuntary strokes and only 11 runs. South Africa were 247 for 5, with McLean on 142, when Statham bowled his next ball. *The Times*: 'If ever a bowler deserved success it was Statham. He put all he had into the penultimate ball before luncheon; its pace surprised McLean and as the batsman offered a frantic back stroke so the ball whipped in off the pitch and hit the middle stump.'

After lunch, as South Africa made their way to 304 all out, Statham was not even granted Tayfield's wicket, although the latter played and missed at him seven times. Statham's final analysis was 27-9-49-2. South Africa had a lead of 171.

May led England to a fighting total of 353, which meant that South Africa needed 183 to win and they began with 35 minutes' batting on the Saturday evening. The pitch was still fast, but it was lasting and England's batting had shown that runs were there. So the visitors were expected to level the series.

But Statham struck at once. His second ball dismissed McGlew lbw, the batsman thinking that the ball was going down the leg side. McGlew had faced three balls, all from Statham, in the match for his pair. Then Goddard snicked a ball from Statham so faintly that the bowler himself did not realize it until Evans appealed. The last ball of the day, from Trueman to Cheetham, was most unfortunate. The batsman received a nasty crack on the left elbow which chipped a bone and put him out of the next two Tests.

But even after these three quick blows, South Africa still had a good chance of victory on the Monday.

The weather was fine when Endean and night-watchman Tayfield went out to the wicket at 11.30am. Statham, with figures of 4-1-8-2 on the Saturday, now proceeded to bowl five consecutive maidens. Hugh Tayfield was at a loss. The ball was swinging late, especially outwards and Tayfield often missed it by a coat of oil. Or he snicked inswingers on to his pads, which saved him from being lbw.

Not until 12.10pm was a run scored off Statham, and this run perhaps stung him. In his next over, three outswingers almost dismissed Endean. The third was played to point where Titmus dived full length and nodded that he had made a fair catch. However, it seems that both umpires were unsighted and Endean stayed.

The first ball of Statham's next over had Tayfield caught by Evans, so at 12.25pm, South Africa were 40 for 3 and Statham had innings figures so far of 11.1-6-10-3. Trueman was also due credit for his bowling. The match was in the balance. But now the weather intervened, even though it had been fine when play began.

Statham refers to 'smog' having developed. *The Times* refers to an uncanny darkness cast by 'a huge black dome of cloud, which can have refrained from bursting only because of some meteorological phenomenon'.

Some felt it was none too soon when the players came off for bad light at 12.30pm and 43 for 3.

Half an hour later, light rain caused the covers to be brought out, but the dark cloud passed over and at 2.30pm play resumed. The pitch had not been appreciably affected and Statham continued bowling after a beneficial rest. Indeed, the next 80 minutes saw him at his best. John Arlott describes him as "bowling with utter accuracy and savage pace to the ridge end" (that is, from the Pavilion End). Incidentally, the 'ridge' (perhaps on the line of an old drain) does not seem to have played a recognized part in this particular match, although it did in the Lord's Test of two years later, and again after that.

At 2.40pm, McLean played half-cock to a ball which Statham describes as of perfect length, and was bowled. Some reports refer to a poor stroke but probably it was an enforced error.

A quarter of an hour later, Statham beat Endean with two outswingers, the second of which produced a catch to Evans, who was in fine form: 63 for 5, all to Statham.

Waite, like Endean, was morally out to Statham several times before, at 3.35pm, Statham had him lbw playing back to a full-length ball. It was in any case a brute of a ball, which came in from the off and also kept slightly low.

Keith was also given a rough passage by Statham. A bumper just missed his head and twice in an over he was nearly caught by Evans. Then he was beaten by a wonderfully held-back slower ball. Statham, as he tired, was varying his pace cleverly. Finally, Keith, a left-hander, snicked a very fast outswinger and was brilliantly caught at first slip by Graveney.

Now South Africa were 78 for 7 and Statham had taken all seven for 31 runs in an unchanged and inspired spell of 22 overs. The *Manchester Guardian* claimed: 'No other bowler in England, one feels, could have achieved this performance today'.

Trueman had been economical, hostile and indeed in Statham's opinion, magnificent but unlucky.

But the *Manchester Guardian* thought that only Statham was patient, energetic and accurate enough to cope with the South Africans' repeated playing and missing.

What of the South African batsmen? Reports suggest that in these difficult circumstances they were slow of footwork and reaction but that they all batted courageously.

After Keith's dismissal, Statham, although he pulled a stomach muscle just before tea, bowled another seven overs for only eight runs. Mansell and Heine refused to succumb until 5pm, when Wardle, who had taken over from Trueman in mid-afternoon, dismissed them both at 111.

Statham had just been given his sweater, so he was about to be rested anyway and must have been nearly exhausted. The match was now over, Cheetham unfortunately being unable to bat. England had won by 71 runs. The South Africans sportingly applauded Statham into the pavilion with, said *The Times*, 'as much admiration as anyone else on the ground'.

Statham's analysis of 29-12-39-7 was the best of his first-class career to that date. It was the result of an unchanged spell throughout the South Africans' innings of three and three-quarter hours. Statham could probably not have achieved this without the two-hour stoppage of play around lunch. As it was, the innings was divided up into four periods, the longest being one and three-quarter hours.

What were Statham's own feelings about his effort? Of course, after the match he felt completely 'drained', and he had the pulled stomach muscle too. But he later wrote, defending his captain: "The man who wanted me to keep bowling was — Statham. Many times the skipper asked me if I wanted to come off, but each time I told him, 'No'. I always felt I was going to get a wicket and I wanted to make the most of it. I can't say I felt exhausted at the time, because I did not. In those circumstances you may get tired, but with wickets falling regularly you always find the strength for a couple more overs. . . and then a couple more. The physical strain must have been pretty great, though, for I pulled a stomach muscle badly enough to keep me out of the Manchester Test. The fault was entirely mine."

Statham thought that, never before in an innings, had he beaten the bat so consistently. Moreover, when he looked back over his completed career he thought this was perhaps his most satisfying performance.

It was one which led *The Times* to express the hope that this Test would always be remembered for Statham's bowling.

Statham reckoned, and onlookers such as Trevor Bailey suspected, that he never felt truly fit again for the rest of the season. After Lord's, he missed one county match and then took eight wickets in Geoff Edrich's benefit match.

Sadly, Statham's injury returned late in that fixture. The next day, he failed a fitness test on his stomach muscles and so had to miss the Manchester Test. England fielded an opening attack of Bedser and Tyson, a unique occasion. The match, dramatic throughout, was won by South Africa by three wickets.

After ten days away from cricket, Statham was ready for the fray again on 16 July, when Leicestershire visited Old Trafford. On the Saturday, Lancashire batted carefully to reach 296 for 5 and on the Monday morning, Hilton was out at 307 for 6, which brought Statham to the wicket. He had permission to go for quick runs.

He hit Jeff Goodwin for three successive fours, with two drives and a cut. In Goodwin's next over, Statham hit 2 sixes, a driven four and a single; thus he reached 29 from the first nine balls he faced. Then he took another single and hit three successive fours off Spencer to reach 42 in 15 minutes.

Munden, left-arm slow, and Lester replaced the pace bowlers, and two more fours took Statham to 50 in 25 minutes. This was a faster 50 than that of Winslow for the South Africans against Lancashire (without Statham) six weeks earlier; Winslow, at one stage, hit 40 off eight consecutive balls he received, but he had begun slowly.

Statham hit three more boundaries to reach 62 in half an hour.

"Then I received a message," he writes, "brought out to me from Washie. It said simply: 'What are you playing at, you fool? Get out.' "

So, next ball, he did, having scored nearly all of a stand of 68 in 30 minutes with Grieves. Washbrook was worried that Statham would tire himself for his bowling and the bowler admits that his captain was probably right. Statham also says that he was robbed of a century! Nevertheless, it was his highest score and indeed remained so.

From 23 balls, he had failed to score off seven and hit the others for 12 fours, 2 sixes and two singles.

Less than half an hour later, Statham opened the bowling and proceeded to take 4 for 34 as Lancashire went on to an innings victory. It was now 19 July and the rest of the season saw no more great deeds from Statham, but (starting in Melbourne) the year of 1955 had already seen many.

The South Africans levelled the series in the Fourth Test at Leeds. Here, deep footholds at the Kirkstall Lane End had caused a broken bone in Adcock's foot, and in South Africa's second innings, Statham was unable to bowl from that end. *Wisden* states that Statham, with figures of 40-10-127-2 in the second innings, 'seemed to lack inspiration in the absence of Tyson,' but overlooks the absence of Trueman. After all, Trueman was Statham's supporter at Lord's. However, in any event, Statham was used to being a lone spearhead for Lancashire (1955 being a prime example) so I feel that at Leeds he was probably simply jaded.

At The Oval, thanks mainly to Lock and Laker, England won to take the series 3-2. In the rubber, Statham took more wickets than any other England bowler and, incidentally, in his four Tests he had opened in turn with Tyson, Trueman, Loader and then Bailey.

In the season, Statham took over a hundred first-class wickets and topped his middle-of-the-table county's averages with a figure of 12.82.

Old Trafford Hat-trick

LET me begin this mention of the 1956 season with Test cricket. Of course, it was Jim Laker's series. One must look wider than the Old Trafford Test and see Laker's figures for the five Tests, which are 283.5-127-442-46, average 9.60. No one has ever approached this domination in an Ashes series.

Thus, clearly, Statham's part against Australia was minor. Indeed, he says that he was mainly a fielder. I will restrict myself to saying that, yes, he did play in the Old Trafford Test, and his contribution to its fame was in the dismissal of Benaud in the first innings, c Statham b Laker 0. The catch was at long on.

For Lancashire, Statham had, by his standards, a typically good, although unexceptional season as his county finished second to Surrey, despite a wet summer in which half their matches were undecided. Indeed, Lancashire twice led the table and were, said *Wisden,* 'a constant threat to the Champions'. But there was as usual no holding Surrey, who in the end won by 20 points.

Most of Statham's own success came at Old Trafford. In the season's first game there, Lancashire proved too strong for Somerset. Statham's main contribution came at around six o'clock on the Monday, when the visitors, 104 in arrears, had to start their second innings. In scoring 11 runs, Somerset lost four wickets, three of them to Statham, and two of those three fell at 0. Next day, he finished with an analysis of 24.1-12-23-4, as Somerset, 148 all out, were beaten by ten wickets.

Lancashire won their next home match, against Glamorgan, by the same margin. The England bowler, admittedly on a wearing pitch, showed up the visitors' second-innings batting. After two even first-innings, Glamorgan began their second knock immediately before lunch on the second day and both Hedges and Pleass were caught in the slips off Statham in the first few minutes.

During the afternoon, the Welshmen 'continued their tame surrender', said the *Western Mail.* Statham had Parkhouse caught hooking a bumper and he bowled two tail-enders, whilst Tattersall (who bowled throughout the innings) and Hilton accounted for the other five. Glamorgan were 52 all out, the fast bowler's analysis being 13-7-13-5, and Lancashire won late that afternoon.

Statham's next appearance at Old Trafford was in June against Middlesex. On the opening day, his county hit an aggressive 341 and late that evening he bowled Jack Robertson for four and had Bill Edrich leg-before for ten. On the second day, Middlesex collapsed, mainly to Tattersall.

In the follow-on, Statham again bowled Robertson (this time for a duck), and had Edrich caught for two. The visitors fought back from 44 for 6 to 112 for 7, but the England bowler ensured an innings victory inside two days by having the last three men caught at the wicket at a cost of two runs. His figures were 5 for 31, giving him 9 for 65 in the match.

On 10 July, Brian Statham took his first hat-trick in first-class cricket. Lancashire had made 248 against Sussex at Old Trafford and then Statham bowled two men without a run on the board. Sussex went on to 110 all out and Lancashire later declared, leaving the visitors to try for 267 in 225 minutes. In his second over, Statham yorked Oakman, who was about to make his Test debut.

Then came lunch and Statham began his second over after the interval by getting Parks lbw. The next ball had Suttle lbw. The third knocked Semmence's leg stump through the air.

Sussex were 29 for 5 and never recovered, so Lancashire kept on Surrey's heels. Statham took 5 for 22, but his best analysis of the season came at its end, in Lancashire's second match against the Australians on 15 August.

For the Australians, this was a depressing return to the scene of Laker's greatest triumph. At the start, the weather was cold, damp and gloomy and it never improved. The pitch was adjacent to the one for the Fourth Test, although greener. In the humid atmosphere, the tourists had to face Statham, and the wind, coming at them from the Stretford end — 'Laker's end'. The light was not good, although at least Old Trafford has long had a reputation for easy sighting of the ball.

The thousand or so people who risked the weather were rewarded with the sight of Statham taking a wicket in his second, third and fourth overs. The last ball of his second over had Rutherford caught at the wicket off an outswinger. His next ball, a fast inswinger, bowled McDonald, but Craig stopped a hat-trick. At noon, Harvey snicked an outswinger to second slip and Statham had figures of 3.3-0-9-3. At 12.15pm, however, rain stopped play, the Australians being 22 for 3. There was further play from 1.15pm to 1.30pm, which took the score to 40 for 3.

Play could restart only at 2.40pm. Colin Smith, although having an erratic day, chipped in with Craig's wicket and Statham bowled Archer first ball with an outswinger: 42 for 5. Burge and Davidson speeded the collapse by playing poor shots to Statham, the former being lbw to an inswinger, the latter brilliantly caught at first slip off an outswinger. It was 3.10pm, Statham had 6 for 22 and the tourists were 57 for 7.

Benaud had hit his team to 86 for 7 when, at 3.25pm, the rain came down. Statham's figures were 12-2-27-6 — and there was no more play in the match.

Brian Statham on his way to Australia and New Zealand and his Test debut, at the age of 20. Statham is pictured at London Airport with Roy Tattersall (left) in January 1951, when the MCC tourists summoned the two Lancashire bowlers as reinforcements. Hulton Picture Company.

Statham putting his back into the job, for England against Australia at Lord's in 1953. Keith Miller watches the ball on its way. Sport & General.

A portrait taken at Lord's in 1954, when Statham was 24 years old. Sport & General.

Statham's flowing follow-through reflects his loose-limbed suppleness. And his performance here, at The Oval in his last match of the 1954 season, lifted him to the top of the national averages. Hulton Picture Company.

Acknowledging the applause at Lord's in 1955, after bowling South Africa to defeat in the Second Test with an analysis of 29-12-39-7, those wickets being the first seven to fall. Applauding in the background are Fred Trueman (centre) and captain Peter May (right). Sport & General.

The hat-trick ball, MCC v Transvaal at Johannesburg, December 1956. Peter Heine is yorked middle-stump, becoming the third consecutive victim, each clean-bowled. The silly mid on is Frank Tyson and the non-striker is Russell Endean. Sport & General.

MCC's congratulations for the hat-trick at Johannesburg. From left to right: Frank Tyson, Denis Compton, Trevor Bailey, Brian Statham, Godfrey Evans, Peter May (nearest camera), Johnny Wardle (shaking hands), Peter Richardson (hidden) and Colin Cowdrey. Sport & General.

Brian Statham the left-handed batsman. He scored over 5,000 runs (average 10.80) including five fifties. Here, at The Oval in June 1958, he hits out against Jim Laker of Surrey. Hulton Picture Company.

Applauded off the field after taking 7 for 57 (in 28 eight-ball overs) during the Second Test against Australia at Melbourne in January 1959. From left to right: Peter Loader, Brian Statham, Peter Richardson and Trevor Bailey. Hulton Picture Company.

Denis Compton presenting Brian Statham with a prize for his performance against South Africa in the Lord's Test of 1960. He took 6 for 63 and 5 for 34 and collected two cases of Cape sherry.
Sport & General.

Captain Colin Cowdrey introduces Peter May, Brian Statham and Fred Truema

er Majesty the Queen during the Lord's Test against Australia in 1961. Sport & General.

Following through, for England against Pakistan at Trent Bridge in 1962. Hulton Picture Company.

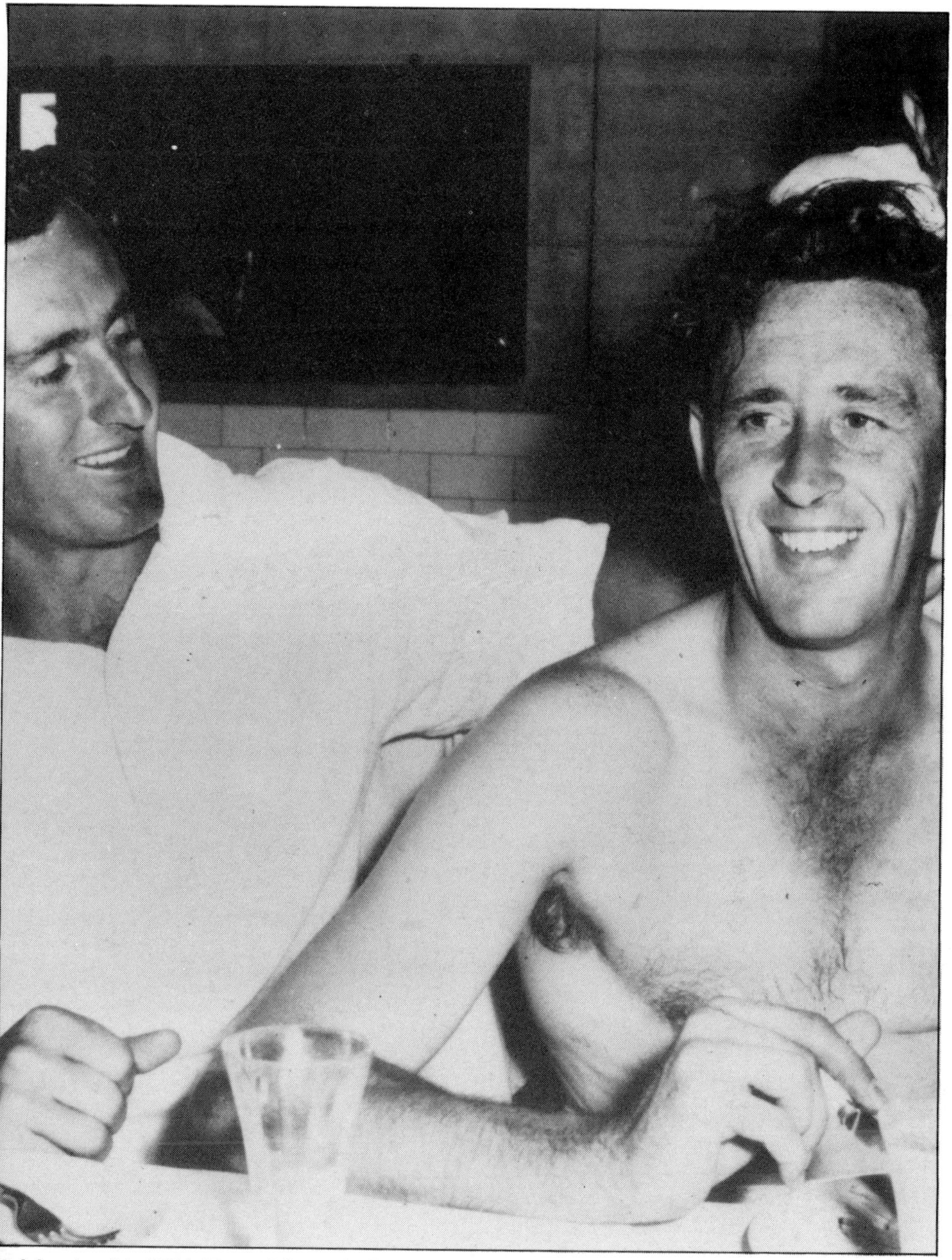

Celebrating his 237th Test wicket, which overtook Alec Bedser's world record. Ted Dexter joins in, over lunch during the Fourth Test against Australia at Adelaide in January 1963. Hulton Picture Company.

Brian Statham still putting his back into it, aged 35, in 1965 when he was the first bowler in the country to reach 100 wickets in the season. Here, at Lord's, with arms whirling, he is in the process of adding six Middlesex wickets to his tally. Sport & General.

Appealing for lbw against Colin Bland of South Africa at The Oval in 1965, when Statham's form for Lancashire earned him a Test recall. Bland was one of his five wickets for 40 in the first innings. From left to right: Ken Barrington, Statham, Colin Cowdrey, Bland, Jim Parks and non-striker 'Tiger' Lance. Hulton Picture Company.

Flying bails — a Brian Statham trademark. Nearly half (over 1,000) of his first-class victims were bowled. The victim here, at Old Trafford in 1968, is Harry Latchman of Middlesex. Wicketkeeper Farokh Engineer celebrates but the slips are still ball-watching. Hallawell Photos.

Appealing for lbw in his farewell appearance, the Roses match at Old Trafford in August 1968. Phil Sharpe is a victim of a spell of 5 for 20 on the first evening. Express Newspapers.

The final wicket of Brian Statham's career. In the second innings of the same match, Yorkshire's Phil Sharpe is again lbw. Engineer supports the bowler's shout. Hallawell Photos.

Later that day, Brian Statham bowls one of the last overs of his career in first-class cricket, but Ray Illingworth is making sure that Statham has indeed taken his last wicket. Hallawell Photos.

Into retirement. At the end of the match, Brian Statham leaves the field for the last time, surrounded by a group of young fans who were not even born when he began his career. Manchester Evening News.

Hat-trick at Johannesburg

AT the start of October 1956, MCC, with Statham, Tyson and Loader as the fast bowlers, set sail for South Africa and reached Cape Town a fortnight later.

Much was hoped for of this series but it was a disappointment, mainly because both sides scored at only 30 runs per 100 balls, or per hour.

The highlights of Brian Statham's contribution to the tour came early. The first first-class game was on 26 October, at Cape Town against Western Province, but on the first day, rain restricted play to the last two hours. The pitch had been covered and was perfect, but Statham struck at once and had figures for the evening of 8-4-10-4, the home side being 39 for 4. The next day he finished with figures of 16-5-26-5, in the opposition's 129 all out, and MCC went on to beat the Currie Cup holders by an innings.

Statham's third match was at the newly-built Wanderers' ground at Johannesburg, an inauspicious location for him because it was 5,700 feet above sea-level and the air was rarefied. Heine and Adcock were used to it, and Loader found that it helped to clear his asthma. But Statham had four matches to play there, and Tyson and Loader had two each, so masseur Harold Dalton decided to have an oxygen cylinder put in the dressing-room for MCC. Statham says that five minutes of oxygen, at each interval in play, solved the breathing problem.

However, his first reaction on 30 November, the first day of the Transvaal match at Johannesburg, had been that it was all he could do to finish each eight-ball over. He took one wicket in the home side's 163 for 5 that day.

The next morning, the Saturday, saw 30,000 people watching in an atmosphere likened to that of a Test. Of course, many were not yet in their seats when, on a true pitch, Statham bowled the day's first over. The eighth ball, a trimmer, bowled Ritchie. Then Wardle bowled a maiden to Endean, and then Statham's first ball of his second over bowled Charnas. Heine had to face the hat-trick ball, but he could not stop Statham's yorker from knocking back the middle stump. The crowd roared and the MCC players surrounded Statham. You cannot get a more personal hat-trick than all clean-bowled.

Late in the day, after tea, the crowd were on their feet again. Replying to 212, MCC had reached 95 for two when May came out to bat. His four first-class innings on the tour thus far had been 162, 118, 124 not out and 206 — four successive centuries, achieved for the first time in South African cricket.

The crowd gave May a generous greeting, but when Heine had him caught at the wicket first ball, the roar, naturally enough, exceeded the one for Statham's hat-trick.

In the end, MCC beat Transvaal, but not before Heine and Adcock had given hints of future trouble for England's batsmen.

In the First Test, also at Johannesburg, Statham took his 100th Test wicket, on 28 December. In the South African second innings, night-watchman Waite faced Statham for his first delivery and could only stun the ball and watch it spin back and dislodge a bail. For his 100 wickets, Statham had bowled some 6,350 balls (about the same as had Wardle when he too reached the milestone during the Fourth Test).

The dismissal of Waite was part of a troublesome evening for South Africa. Soon afterwards, Statham bowled Endean with such a fine leg-cutter, pitching about middle stump and hitting the off stump, that the batsman acknowledged it with a wave. South Africa by then were 25 for 5 and their subsequent 72 all out (Bailey 5 for 20) gave England victory.

But South Africa came back strongly later in the rubber, which ended with two wins for each side. *Wisden* summarized Statham's part in the tour by saying that he 'had days when he looked the best fast bowler in the world but was sometimes worried by injuries and towards the end he lost his snap'.

The first injury was a legacy from Lancashire's last county match of the previous summer, when he had torn the fibres above the Achilles tendon in his right foot. On 1 February he strained a lower abdomen muscle and then had to miss the Fifth Test because of a bruised little right toe.

But, having returned from South Africa in March, he was fit to play in Lancashire's first match on 1 May, at Oxford University.

Rout at Coventry

STATHAM played a notable part in Lancashire's first county match of 1957, a victory at Taunton, by taking 5 for 31 and 3 for 46, all eight victims being bowled.

On Saturday, 18 May, Lancashire were top of the table as they took the field against Warwickshire at Coventry. It had rained overnight, but the pitch was completely protected. The weather was cold when Statham opened with a maiden. Then he changed ends in order to have the wind behind him.

Conditions were made for seam bowling, the ball always moving sharply off the spongy turf. Some deliveries rose, some kept low. Back-foot play was soon seen to be perilous, but few batsmen were courageous enough to come right forward to Statham.

Wharton took the first wicket and in his first five overs Statham had no wicket for six runs. In his sixth over, after a single to Gardner, Statham dismissed both M.J.K.Smith and Townsend with the score at 18. Wolton took four runs off Statham before, in the latter's next over, he was bowled. Statham had taken three wickets while conceding four runs, and had 3 for 11 overall.

Wharton took his second wicket and Warwickshire were 23 for 5 after an hour. At 32, Gardner glanced Statham fine and low to Collins, who took the catch ankle-high; three runs later Statham had Singh caught at mid on. The home side were now 35 for 7 and Statham had taken 5 for 20 in ten overs, of which the last five had produced 5 for 14.

With an hour and a quarter gone, it now seemed that Washbrook was going to rest Statham but he changed his mind. The bowler was finally given a rest with figures of 16-4-33-5 just before Warwickshire went in to lunch at 64 for 7. He was generously applauded by the small crowd.

During the interval, Statham told the *Manchester Evening News* reporter that it was "no use bowling fast out there," which perhaps meant that the conditions warranted his slowing up a shade and letting the ball do the work. This might also explain *Wisden's* comment that Statham made 'splendid use of his faster ball'.

He was back after lunch and in another 16 balls knocked back Carter's off stump, bowled Bannister and had Hollies caught. So he had taken eight wickets in a first-class innings for the first time: 18.4-6-34-8.

Lancashire now gained a lead of nearly 200, thanks to Washbrook's innings — and Statham's. The bowler came in to join his captain at 166 for 7 with the ball still moving a lot off the turf, upon which rain was starting to fall. The rain was quite heavy during the first half of this partnership and, indeed, there was a half-hour stoppage. The ball was difficult for the bowlers to handle, but when Statham straight drove and cover drove boundaries, Washbrook joined in the applause. The pair added 97 in 85 minutes and the bowler reached the fourth 50 of his career before Bannister bowled him for 53, which included five fours.

In Warwickshire's second innings, the wet ground caused Statham foothold trouble, but he overcame this, to the disappointment of the batsmen. In the damp conditions, he made the ball both swing in the air and deviate off the pitch. He made Gardner play and miss before bowling him middle stump, and had Horner at a loss for three balls before trapping him lbw, playing back. When Mike Smith was caught at the wicket, Warwickshire were 12 for three, all three to Statham at a cost of seven runs.

Two runs later, Wolton spooned a ball from Statham to mid wicket and Greenhough ran from silly mid on to take a diving catch. Statham's last ten balls had now produced four wickets for five runs. At 31, Townsend was caught at mid on and Statham had thus dismissed half the side. When Singh was caught at cover and Ibadulla at the wicket, the home team were 37 for 7, and Statham had taken all seven at a cost of 22 runs in ten overs.

Although he had never before taken more than ten wickets in a first-class match, Statham had now captured 15 — the first Lancashire bowler to do so for over 20 years. All-rounder Len Hopwood had taken 15 Worcestershire wickets in 1934 at Blackpool.

Statham continued to bowl, although he was tiring, and Spooner hit him for four fours in quick succession. It was left to Greenhough to dismiss Spooner and two of the tail-enders, to give Lancashire an innings victory inside two days. This kept them at the top of the table.

Statham's second-innings analysis was 17-2-55-7, bowling

unchanged, as indeed he had in the first innings, except for one over from Greenhough.

His match return (at one stage 15 for 56) was 15 for 89, the best by any Lancashire bowler since Harry Dean took 17 for 91 with left-arm spin in July 1913. That had been against Yorkshire on a 'sticky dog' at Aigburth in a non-Championship but first-class match arranged to celebrate the visit of King George V to Liverpool. A sudden change from rain to sunshine had caused Dean to arrive late for that match, but in those conditions he soon made up for lost time.

To find better match figures than Statham's for a Lancashire fast bowler, one had to go back, not to McDonald, but to Walter Brearley in 1905. He took 17 for 137 against Somerset at Old Trafford.

Ten days after the match at Coventry, Statham played in the First Test against the West Indies at Edgbaston. The record stand of 411 by May and Cowdrey, combating Ramadhin, made it famous.

Statham's partner at Edgbaston was Trueman. This had been the case only four times during the first half of Statham's Test career, but from now on it was the case on all but four occasions.

There were several reasons for this development. Tyson and Loader, although they had been selected for South Africa at the expense of Trueman, could not compete with the latter's 40 wickets for Yorkshire by 26 May and this was the immediate reason.

Second, after 1957, Trueman was back in the selectors' favour for tours abroad, having missed two, partly as a result of controversy in the West Indies in 1953-4.

Third, events continued to suggest that Tyson's *annus mirabilis* was indeed just that. The Australian pitches of 1954-5 had been of unrivalled pace and English players never saw such again, even in Australia. Tyson's home pitches at Northampton were amongst the most lifeless in the country and, sadly, they took their toll of him. Indeed, Hutton had warned Tyson that the latter's talents could be blunted there. With a heel injury and an ankle injury contributing, Tyson found a place in only two Tests after 1956-7. He retired in 1960 at the age of 30. In 1957, he did take 100 wickets — for the only time — but he was denied a Test place by Trueman and either Statham or Loader.

Peter Loader, in fact, kept the Statham-Trueman combination apart for part of this and the next two series. This was because

Loader took his chances well when either of the other two was injured, so that he retained his place for a while.

Following Edgbaston, Statham opened with Trueman at Lord's and at Nottingham. The latter saw, according to John Arlott, the 'first major success' of the Statham-Trueman partnership. England, one up, had made 619 for 6 declared and West Indies started their reply with 295 for 3 by Saturday evening.

The Monday and Tuesday saw a real battle. Statham and Trueman, according to *The Times*, never spared themselves for a single moment; when one flagged, the other came to his rescue.

Laker also bowled heroically but it was extra hard work for these three because Bailey was the only other front-line bowler selected, and he ricked his back. This meant that Bailey bowled only 12 low-key overs during the West Indies' second innings, when the visitors staged a great fight-back.

The first hour of Monday's play belonged to Trueman, who in seven overs took 5 for 11. Although covered, the pitch, especially in the eyes of the West Indians, had been freshened by a weekend thunderstorm which followed a heatwave. The ball did move off the seam, although there was only one word for the pitch, even on the fifth day — perfect, certainly for an English one.

Statham bowled well in support of Trueman, but in 28.4 overs in the first innings he had only Ramadhin's wicket. Worrell, who carried his bat for 191, drove Statham for three fours during the last-wicket stand.

At lunchtime, West Indies followed on almost 250 runs in arrears. At three o'clock, Statham produced a fine ball which came back from the off to bowl the tiring Worrell. The visitors collapsed to 89 for 5, of which the fast bowlers had two each, Statham having bowled Weekes with a trimmer. But 'Collie' Smith and Atkinson took the score to 175 for 5 overnight, and the Tuesday brought a third successive playing day of real sweat for the three England bowlers.

They had to put up with an uncommonly fine pitch, the hot weather, Bailey's absence and three dropped catches — and the wonderful batting of Smith supported by his captain, Goddard.

Soon after midday, Statham, with the new ball, had Atkinson caught at the wicket and at 12.30pm the last capable batsman, Goddard, snicked the same bowler. Evans went for a straightforward catch in front of first slip but perhaps tried to celebrate too early and dropped it. Statham regards this as one of the few important errors of Evans' career; it helped to demoralize England and Goddard went on to add 154 with Smith.

Soon Smith became, in Statham's words, "one of the few players to hit me for six." This was no ordinary six. It was hit off the back foot, and the new ball went over the bowler's head, over the sight-screen, and on to the pavilion roof. Smith was in the 90s at the time! And the West Indies had not yet cleared their arrears. But the batsman, though still just short of his century, found time to grin at Statham.

Play having started at 11 o'clock, Statham and Trueman were, said *The Times*, 'dreadfully weary', even by lunch. The previous day, they had bowled 50 overs between them. At 2.30pm, however, Bailey, was able to help out by bowling at half-pace, but Smith and Goddard stayed until 4.50pm when Statham had the latter caught by Evans, with the visitors ahead by 101 and play to finish at 6.30pm; might England still win?

Even though the hero of the innings was out for 168 at about five o'clock, Ramadhin held England up until, when Statham bowled Gilchrist, the home side were left with an hour in which to score an impossible 121.

Statham's second innings analysis was 41.2-12-118-5, so that he had bowled 70 overs in the match. This was the most he ever bowled in one Test, and into the bargain it was a follow-on situation. He says he never recovered his top form that season, but he does not blame his England captain, May, who had little choice.

Statham was injured for the Fourth Test, and his replacement, Loader, did the hat-trick in taking 6-36 in the West Indies' first innings. For the Test at The Oval, Loader kept his place. England won both matches.

Going back to Statham's season with Lancashire, two more performances are worthy of mention. Shortly before the Nottingham Test, he had played at Old Trafford against Somerset on 26 June. Lancashire's results, incidentally, had already fallen away and Surrey were yet again marching ahead.

The pitch had been protected from overnight drizzle. But when Somerset began their reply at the start of the second day, bad light contributed to their making two runs in half an hour. In that time,

Statham had made a ball rear up and injure Alley's finger, the batsman retiring hurt; Wharton took the first wicket, and another kicker from Statham had Tripp caught behind. Later, Statham almost had Wight caught in the gully before he retired after just over an hour with figures of 10-7-4-1. Somerset's total then was only ten, which also speaks well for Wharton and the spinners.

After lunch, Statham came back and had both Wight and the returning Alley caught at slip, and Stephenson lbw: a spell of 2.4-1-5-3 since the interval. When Jim Hilton (formerly of Lancashire) and Ken Palmer were caught by the close field, Statham since lunch had taken 5 for 7, and he finished with 18-9-19-6 out of the visitors' 90 all out. He had 10-4-12-3 in the follow-on total of 74 all out as Lancashire won in two days.

At the end of August, Warwickshire came to Old Trafford and in their second innings Statham reminded the visitors of the Coventry match. On a rain-affected pitch he dismissed both openers for next to nothing, bowled M.J.K.Smith for 30, and bowled two further batsmen for ducks. This gave him 5-16 of the visitors' overnight 104 for 7. The next morning Spooner was caught off a sharp riser from Statham, who finished with 6 for 22, and Lancashire went on to win with time in hand.

The last county match of the season followed, at Blackpool, where Statham had match figures on a lively pitch of 9 for 60 against Worcestershire, and Lancashire's victory gave them sixth place in the final table.

Statham topped his county's Championship averages with 100 wickets at 12.57 each, and moreover was second only to Lock of the major bowlers in the national averages.

Lucky Thirteen

THE rainy summer of 1958 was one of good fortune at county level for Statham in that a bowler of high promise was found to partner him regularly. Behind the scenes, Lancashire moved quickly to specially register a player from Staffordshire whom they had shown an interest in.

Ken Higgs, aged 21, did not even start with Lancashire Second XI but, after playing in a friendly and in the two University matches, went straight into Lancashire's first Championship game, against Hampshire at Old Trafford. *Wisden* described the new bowler as possessing accuracy and the ability to move the ball either way, though not real pace.

Statham and Higgs opened against Hampshire and between them picked up five first-innings wickets, although the visitors gained a useful lead.

The second afternoon belonged to Higgs, with a week's first-class experience, and to Statham. Higgs had to bowl against the wind, but he swept all before him. He took 7 for 36 and Statham had 3 for 14 as the pair bowled unchanged through Hampshire's 50 all out! Twelve points were duly collected; so the match was a good omen for the two bowlers. But Statham, looking back, praises Higgs for not becoming over-confident and for always remaining willing to learn.

In 1967 A.A.Thomson wrote that "Statham has been reckoned luckier than Trueman ever was in having virtually the ideal opening partner in Higgs." Higgs did have a few disappointing seasons on the way, but Statham acknowledges the valuable support and help which his partner provided. Statham was perhaps particularly grateful because Lancashire, as a team, had a barren time during most of the period of this partnership.

At Whitsun 1958, Headingley was the scene of the Roses match. The weather prevented any play until 4.20pm on the Saturday, when Statham opened with two uneventful overs on a pitch which seemed rather wet for speed bowling. But his third over contained three balls which reared up and just missed the bat, and Lowson, the recipient, perhaps shaken, fell to Wharton (Higgs was not playing) in the next over.

Statham's first ball to Vic Wilson was a late outswinger which led to a catch at first slip. Five runs later, Ken Taylor was caught at the wicket off a nasty lifter from the same bowler, which touched the batsman's glove and maybe even his cap. At the same score, Padgett was taken by second slip off another Statham outswinger: 13 for 4.

Close played a few good strokes but Statham made him turn an inswinger to short leg, where Trueman, playing forward, was also caught: 24 for 6, five of them to Statham. Illingworth led a slight recovery but with Statham having Wardle caught high up in the gully and with Tattersall taking two wickets, Yorkshire were 64 for 9 soon after six o'clock. The acting captain, Wardle, then declared.

Statham had bowled unchanged for an hour and three-quarters as the pitch had gradually dried, his analysis being 14-8-16-6. All his victims had been caught close to the wicket — the fielding had been brilliant. A.A.Thomson thought that the batsmen facing Statham had "offered catches to slip and short leg as though snicking were some virus epidemic."

The *Manchester Guardian* reported that some '5,000 sorely-harrowed Yorkshiremen cheered Statham when he left the field as if he had been born and bred their own. No Lancashire man received more eloquent tribute.'

Lancashire's batsmen in the last 15 minutes of play defused Wardle's declaration by making seven runs without loss. On Whit Monday, 18,000 people saw Lancashire prepare the way for an eight-wicket victory the next day.

In the following game, against Surrey at Old Trafford, Statham again took six wickets in the first innings, though this time for 78 runs. The dominant entry in the score-book read 'May, bowled Statham 174'. In the final innings of the match the Surrey bowlers, helped by a shower, dismissed the home team for 27, which is still Lancashire's second lowest total ever — but, as we shall see, Statham redressed the balance in the record books before the season was over.

Trueman and Loader appeared in the First Test against New Zealand on 5 June, and in the next two Tests, so that they combined in five consecutive Tests altogether. While the First Test was in progress, Statham played for his county at Old Trafford. Rain early and late on the Saturday limited play to three hours and ten minutes which saw Middlesex make only 116 for 3. Statham, on a slow but not treacherous pitch, reduced the batsmen to statues. Before lunch he bowled nine overs for three runs and continued afterwards with another five overs for two runs. Three more overs later in the day and a further three on Monday morning produced six runs so that he finished with an analysis of 20-11-11-1; no one had hit a boundary off him. The match, with more rain, was, of course, a draw.

A month later, during the Third Test, Statham played against Leicestershire at Old Trafford and perhaps his performance regained him his Test place.

On the Saturday, rain delayed the start and had softened the pitch, but Leicestershire chose to bat. In Statham's first over, Hallam, with bat aloft, left a ball alone, but it broke back and hit his off stump. After lunch, Statham, by means of movement off the pitch, was chiefly responsible for Leicestershire's collapse from 47 for 2 to 99 all out. Willie Watson, having survived a fiendish yorker from Statham, scored half their total.

In this period Statham bowled two men, had one leg-before and had two caught at the wicket, all for 16 runs. His innings analysis was 16.5-6-20-6.

Lancashire replied with 213 for 9 by Monday lunchtime in spite of conditions which, early that morning, resembled a sea-fog. Against the odds, wicketkeeper Alan Wilson and Tattersall now each made the highest scores of their careers. In better than even time, they put on 105 runs, by hook or by crook. The *Manchester Guardian* reporter was amused in the same way as he was by custard-pie sequences in silent films. The crowd, of course, enjoyed the fun and when Tattersall, nearing his 50, padded up to a ball, they accused him of having been watching Washbrook! At 3.50pm Tattersall was out and the pair — whose career batting averages were each in single figures — were given quite an ovation.

Tea was taken, and Lancashire, with a lead of 219, then had two hours 20 minutes' bowling left on this second day. Statham made good use of it and at one stage the score-card read:

Leicestershire		
Hallam	b Statham	0
Watson	b Statham	8
Lester	b Statham	9
Revill	not out	1
Gardner	b Statham	0
Diment	lbw b Statham	0
Julian	not out	0
Total	**(5 wickets)**	**18**

But this does not reveal that Statham achieved a hat-trick. He bowled Watson off stump, then with the next two balls bowled Gardner and had Diment lbw. It was the third hat-trick of his career, all within about 18 months. He took two more wickets later and finished with an analysis of 16-2-44-7 as the visitors were all out for 87, to give Lancashire an innings win before the day was over. His match figures were 13 for 64, and eight of his victims had been bowled.

His form was confirmed by a second-innings analysis in the following match at Derby of 19.5-7-21-5. The last of those victims, Gladwin, was the bowler's 1,000th in first-class cricket, well over 7,000 overs being involved in reaching this milestone.

On 16 July, Statham made his third appearance in a Gentlemen v Players fixture, and on 24 July he was recalled to the England team for the Fourth Test against New Zealand. He partnered Trueman, at Manchester, and England won again. During this match, MCC chose the tour party for Australia and it included Statham.

His next match was at Blackpool, where Gloucestershire were the visitors and batted first. His second ball was an outswinger which Young touched to the wicketkeeper. His sixth ball rose and Nicholls was only able to play it on to his stumps: 2 for 2. Forty minutes later, Graveney was only five when Statham beat him by movement to have him lbw. When Statham bowled Carpenter, had Milton leg-before, and bowled Mortimore, Gloucestershire were 71 for 6, all the wickets falling to Statham. And Grieves had missed a chance off his bowling.

In all, Statham bowled for an hour and 40 minutes, that is for almost the whole of the innings of 96 all out, and finished, after bowling Meyer, with an analysis of 22-8-29-7, his second best to that date. Lancashire went on to win by an innings.

A week later Lancashire played at Cardiff. Put in to bat on a damp pitch, they nevertheless scored 351, to which Glamorgan replied at the end of the first day by losing three wickets — two of them to Statham — while scoring five runs.

Next day, play was delayed by rain until 5.30pm. Out on the field, Bob Barber (captain in the absence of Washbrook) discussed the conditions with Statham. It seemed too slippery for genuinely fast bowling, but Statham opened, with what was initially a trial over. Tattersall bowled at the other end; then Statham continued, and met with immediate reward.

He bowled four successive batsmen while the score crept up to 13 for 7. In the process he sent Ward's bail nearly 40 yards, took his 100th wicket of the season and took his figures to six wickets for seven runs. With Tattersall chipping in, Glamorgan sank to 15 for 9.

There were ironies here in that Glamorgan's lowest-ever score of 22 (in 1924) had been made against Lancashire, and Lancashire themselves had been all out for 27 earlier in 1958. Now Lancashire had to be satisfied with conceding 11 runs for the last wicket and with Glamorgan being all out for 26. Statham's analysis was 16-9-12-6, but the match itself was then rained off, there being no play on the final day.

Rain also spoilt the Fifth Test, but by the end of the season Statham had taken more Championship wickets (112) and more first-class wickets (134) than in any previous summer. He led his county's Championship averages with the notable figure of 11.40 and was third nationally, behind Les Jackson and Tony Lock. An end-of-season friendly against Yorkshire had boosted his figures — he took 5 for 8 and said it was very friendly!

And this was his most economical season, in that he only conceded, during nearly 900 overs, an average of 1.84 runs per over.

Losing Ashes Battle

STATHAM, Trueman, Tyson and Loader formed the fast-bowling contingent of the MCC team, captained by Peter May, which sailed on the *SS Iberia* for Australia in mid-September 1958.

From the first match, at Perth, onwards it became clear that the pitches this time were tame compared to the truly fast ones of the 1954-5 tour. The situation on Hutton's tour had arisen because the constituent couch grass had been removed specifically to enliven the pitches; but this also caused them to crack in the hot sun, so the couch grass was later restored.

Trueman was on his first tour to Australia and his appetite had been whetted not only by stories of the 1954-5 pitches but also by Herbert Sutcliffe's memories. But, unfortunately for the English fast bowlers, Australian pitches had never been so easy-paced as they now turned out to be.

Tyson, who expounds the couch-grass theory, and Trueman both compared the Australian pitches in 1958-9 to those in England in respect of their docility.

With MCC withdrawing Wardle's invitation for disciplinary reasons and not choosing a replacement, it transpired that the tourists' attack on such pitches was ill-balanced. This was a disadvantage the team could have done without, because for them the tour was to be full of disappointments.

Statham found his form in his second match, against Victoria at Melbourne, starting on 7 November. By the Saturday evening, MCC had scored 396 and Victoria, watched by 30,000 people, had replied with 119 for 3. *The Times* commented that lifeless pitches were drawing the teeth of England's attack; that Statham and Loader had found it hard to raise the ball above stump height; that it was hard to believe that a fast bowler would get another wicket in the match; and that, left to the fast bowlers, the result was bound to be a draw.

On the Monday, the third day of this four-day game, the shaven pitch still gave Statham, in *Wisden's* words, not the slightest encouragement. *The Times* reported that Laker and Lock were played with ease, that Bailey strove in vain and that Loader's pace did not worry even the number-eight Victoria batsman.

In spite of all this, Statham succeeded. *The Times* said he towered in stature above all the other bowlers. In his second over, his fourth ball had Shaw lbw to a break-back, his sixth beat Potter for speed and bowled him and his seventh forced Maddocks, hurriedly, to almost play on. When Statham had bowled four overs for five runs, Cowdrey chose, for no obvious reason, to give him a long rest. But no one else obtained a wicket, and the Lancashire player, apart from bowling two overs after lunch, passively watched a stand of 90 carry Victoria to 213 for 5, when the new ball was taken at 3pm.

Now Statham, in the words of the *Manchester Guardian* reporter, 'by some exercise of art that seemed to elude both his colleagues and opponents, on this dry, hot, dazzlingly sunny day, contrived to whip several deliveries with the new ball now slightly into, now away from the bat'. His yorker was also lethal, and he varied his pace cleverly, though the ball did not swing.

Although Huntington and Maddocks had confidently put on 100, Statham in his second over bowled the latter, who cut a ball on to his stumps. The *Manchester Guardian* said that 'unbelievably' the ball had lifted. In his next over, Statham moved one in to bowl Huntington for 73, and in his fourth yorked Meckiff and Kline. Loader took the last wicket without addition, so Victoria had collapsed to 252 all out. Statham had figures of 6 for 25 on the day in ten eight-ball overs, and an innings analysis of 17-2-47-7, six bowled and one lbw.

His feat helped MCC to win off the penultimate ball of the match, Lock taking 6-74 on the last day.

This tour was bedevilled by a throwing controversy, chiefly in the Tests — where Meckiff took 17 wickets at 17.17 apiece — but to some degree in most matches. Queensland indeed seemed to be, perhaps thanks to the influence of their captain, Ray Lindwall, the only major state team with no doubtful bowler.

Tyson, Trueman and the Australians Keith Miller and Jack Fingleton, to name four experts, would have no-balled Meckiff at least on occasion; but Tyson's opinion that the destination of the Ashes was not altered by the 'throwers' was widely held, for example by Statham. The fine bowling of Benaud and Davidson was also widely acknowledged as being crucial.

Statham has written a worthwhile summary and I intend to sign off this topic with it:

> "Unfortunately no complaint was made to the Australian Board of Control, although the majority of our boys thought Meckiff threw from the first time they saw him. Most of the Australian players told me they thought he threw. Meckiff himself did not believe he threw. He genuinely believed he bowled as straight and true as anybody and a nicer lad you could not wish to meet.
>
> "A complaint should have gone in during this First Test but it was decided not to bother. Meckiff was so erratic the English batsmen did not think he would be a great threat in the series. They thought the same about Rorke, but they continued to experience difficulty in picking up the ball from the hand. They could not judge the flight.
>
> "This was the cause of the trouble when Meckiff suddenly started letting it go straight and became such a menacing wicket-taker during the rest of the tour. By that time it was too late to complain. It would have looked as if we were squealing just because we were getting beaten."

The First Test ended in a comfortable Australian win and on 31 December Statham was back at Melbourne for the Second Test. Loader partnered him as in the First Test. Trueman, although his nine South Australian wickets suggested he had recovered from back trouble, was left out, as was Tyson.

The pitch was faster and better-grassed than the one for the Victoria game, but it was described by Statham as perfect for Harvey while the latter was making a brilliant 167. England scored 259 and Australia went in at 3.10pm on the second day. Statham dismissed Burke for three when the batsman offered no stroke to a ball which came in from outside the off stump to hit it. But Harvey hit 10 fours in taking Australia to 96 for 1 overnight.

For the third day, 40,000 people arrived for the start and the final attendance was 71,295. Australia could score only slowly but did not lose a wicket until just after lunch when Statham had

McDonald caught at first slip. Harvey (140 not out) and O'Neill took the score to 216 for 2 at tea, after which the new ball was taken.

But now 39 runs came in 40 minutes so that at 5pm Australia were 255 for 2. Harvey had just taken 12 off a Loader over, and not only the bowlers were looking tired but the fielders too. Then Statham produced a very fast ball, just short of a length, and it lifted just outside the off stump. O'Neill, with a shot of aggressive intent, could only snick the ball to Evans, who accepted the catch, albeit like a juggler.

Loader, 'on the instant translated' by the breakthrough according to the *Manchester Guardian,* now bowled Harvey and had Simpson leg-before for a duck. Statham beat Benaud by pace to have him also lbw for a duck, and his very next ball all but dismissed Davidson the same way. Australia were 262 for 6, only three runs ahead. Statham and Loader had taken four wickets for seven runs in 25 minutes, and the *Manchester Evening News* reporter said: 'Where Statham found the stamina to "go to town" as he did, I'll never know', and the same could have been said of Loader. Australia finished the day at 282 for 6, and Statham's overall figures were 21-4-45-4.

The following morning, the England fast bowlers completed Australia's collapse. At 295, Statham moved a ball away from Mackay who was thus caught at the wicket. In his next over, he sent Davidson's off stump flying and hit Meckiff's with the next ball but one. This was a spell of three wickets without cost in two overs, and Australia were 300 for 9. Grout hit Statham over mid on for four, but paid for it with the next ball, which struck him on the toe painfully. Loader took the last wicket at 308.

Statham had 3 for 12 off seven overs that morning, for an innings analysis of 28-6-57-7. The huge crowd saw the Australian batsmen, as well as the English team, applaud him as he led the way through the pavilion gate.

Australia's lead had been restricted to 49 and England began their second innings at about lunchtime with some optimism. Statham says the pitch that afternoon was perfect.

He had a shower and put his feet up in the dressing-room for a rest. Later in the afternoon he was disturbed by an exhortation to don his pads. He thought it was a leg-pull, but in fact England had collapsed to 44 for 5, and were 75 for 8 when Statham had to go out to bat soon after tea. In England's 87 all out, Meckiff took 6 for 38.

Trevor Bailey regards Statham as the most imperturbable fast bowler he saw, but this was one occasion when the Lancashire player was ruffled. He had bowled brilliantly and had earned a spell of lounging. Instead, as Bailey says, Statham "had to bat and bowl again the same day. He was not amused."

The Australians needed only 39 to win even though only a few hours earlier England had had reasons for optimism. Statham's dismissal of McDonald lbw at the end of the day was academic; on the Monday morning, Australia went 2-0 up in the rubber.

The home team never looked back and, by drawing the next Test and winning the fourth to lead 3-0, regained the Ashes. England had won the three previous series, which was unprecedented in this century, but now the tide was turned.

After losing the Ashes at Adelaide, MCC played a one-day game against a Victoria Country XI. This was at Wangaratta on Saturday, 7 February. After providing popular entertainment there, the tourists had to move on about 125 miles to Wagga Wagga in New South Wales for a similar fixture on the Monday.

They travelled in a convoy of cars and Statham and Loader were passengers in the last car, which also contained three Wangaratta businessmen. Towards the end of the journey, at a place called The Rock, a tyre burst and their car hit a post on a bend in darkness and overturned.

Statham and Loader crawled out covered in petrol and suffering from minor injuries and shock. The three businessmen were only shaken.

Statham had a bruised neck and shoulder and Loader had a cut head and a cut right elbow. Statham was given massage and Loader three stitches in his arm, after which local treatment they completed their journey.

Neither player took any further part in the tour and both flew home before the visit to New Zealand.

The part Statham had played was summarized by *Wisden* thus: 'The England bowlers were usually in the unhappy position of having few runs to play with, but no one could have bowled more wholeheartedly than Statham. He was magnificent in the first innings of the Second Test at Melbourne, and in the three other Tests in which he played he bowled fast and accurately although not always meeting with the success he deserved.'

This last comment can be illustrated by the first ball of the Fourth Test at Adelaide. Laker was injured so for the first and only time Statham, Trueman and Tyson all played in the same Test. The pitch was the normal Adelaide batting paradise, but May reasonably thought that the only chance of his fast bowlers dismissing Australia twice and thus of saving the Ashes was to put Australia in.

Statham bowled the first ball to McDonald, and Tyson and Lindwall are two witnesses who have since referred to it in writing. Lindwall said: "May and the England players jumped with hope and expectation when the first ball from Statham cut back sharply from the off and just went over the top of Colin McDonald's middle stump. It was a beautiful ball and deserved a wicket, but it was the only ball in the whole match that showed any life." Tyson emphasized that McDonald went on to score a match-winning 170. Here I should add that the batting of McDonald, O'Neill and Harvey in the series contributed much to England's downfall.

So it was an ill-starred tour for England, who also lost the Fifth Test and thus went down in the rubber by 4-0. Only two Australian sides had ever won an Ashes series so thoroughly, and they were the great sides of 1920-21 and 1948.

All the England players, from May downwards, had a difficult tour. Statham says controversies burdened the whole team. If it was the batsmen who suffered the more from these, the bowlers too had their share of ill-luck. For Statham, the car accident was part of that share; but it was at least fortunate that at the time of the crash no one was smoking. Perhaps Statham and Loader, looking back, prefer that piece of luck to any which they, or England, might have had instead on the field of play.

Topping the National Averages

'THE sun shone brightly, even at Old Trafford', wrote A.A.Thomson, which was a Yorkshireman's way of saying that 1959 was one of the finest summers anyone could recall. The country's highest temperature reached 82°F in May and 96°F in July, and then came the warmest August since 1947.

It was dry, too, and in the period May to September England and Wales had only half the normal rainfall, which was unprecedented and was a great contrast to the previous summer.

With its dry, firm pitches, it was 'not a summer for bowlers', said *Wisden*. But, as we shall see, that did not put Statham off his stride. As for the batsmen, they made hay while the sun shone, and whereas in 1958 only three players all told had reached 2,000 runs, three from Lancashire alone did so in 1959.

On 9 May at Fenner's, Statham played his first match since the accident, and proved himself fit by bowling five Cambridge batsmen in an analysis which read 18.4-6-28-6.

On 27 May at Gravesend, he met with sterner opposition. Cowdrey, although he invited Statham to stay at his house, did not extend his hospitality to the field of play. He came in at 12.45 on the second morning, Kent then being 24 for 2 in reply to Lancashire's 316. Statham bowled the first ball to him, and it was a nasty inswinger of perfect length. Cowdrey middled it nonchalantly. However, he did take a quarter of an hour to get off the mark; Higgs was also bowling well, and there was a degree of lift early on from the otherwise flawless pitch.

Soon after lunch, Cowdrey made a caressing off drive against Statham which in fact went away like a bullet for four. He progressed steadily (though a straight hit off Dyson brought him six) to his 50 in two hours at 3.25pm. Then Greenhough proved expensive and just after tea Cowdrey was in the 90s when Pretlove was out at 188 for 4.

In the next hour and 20 minutes (which saw his century, including 15 fours, at five o'clock) Cowdrey scored 73 out of a 100 stand with Pettiford. The new ball was taken during this stand, but Cowdrey was unmoved; 52 runs were hit off it in half an hour.

At the close, the England batsman, having nearly scored a hundred since tea, had made 176 out of Kent's 305 for 6, and he had hit 13 fours since five o'clock. Moreover, the bowling was reported as being good.

On the last morning, rapid scoring by Kent might have made a result possible, but Cowdrey was at last lbw to Statham when two short of his double century. It seems that the batsman may have been unlucky in the decision. But if the crowd were disappointed at Cowdrey's dismissal for 198 and at the tame draw which transpired, they had already been treated to a classic innings, and to a run-a-minute average during Cowdrey's five and a half hours at the wicket.

Statham's figures of 36-6-121-3 were among the most expensive he ever had; but his poker-faced comment on his England colleague's innings was, as quoted by John Kay: "Oh, he was just making me pay for bed and breakfast."

Ten days later Statham played in the First Test against India at Nottingham. England were to achieve the rare feat of a 5-0 win in the series — it was no use looking to the weather for a draw in 1959.

John Arlott says that this rubber established the Trueman-Statham partnership, and that, but for injury to Statham, the pair would have played in every Test. Tyson, Loader and Bailey had played their last Tests, which ties in nicely with Arlott's main statement.

At Nottingham, England began the way they meant to go on by scoring 422 and then dismissing India for 206. The follow-on started in mid-afternoon on the Saturday. A Statham outswinger to the left-handed Contractor had the opener well caught, low at second slip for a duck. But then the bowler had to endure three missed catches in the slips. The captain, May, missed two difficult chances at third slip, the first being from Roy and the second, shoulder-high, from Umrigar; then Cowdrey failed to catch Manjrekar.

But after tea, Statham produced a ball which came in so much that it bowled Umrigar while he was shouldering arms. On the

Monday, when India resumed at 96 for 3, rain contributed to there being only a very small crowd; play had to stop from 12.40 to 1.20pm. After lunch Statham had the advantages of a new ball and a freshened pitch, and India (with Borde absent and Nadkarni handicapped, in each case owing to a hand injury) did not last long.

Statham bowled the left-handed Nadkarni behind his legs; he had the captain, Gaekwad, on the back foot to an outswinger, caught in the gully; and he had Gupte caught by May. Trueman joined in, and India were beaten by an innings. Statham's analysis was 21-10-31-5.

The Lord's Test followed. The 'ridge' had influenced the 1957 Test; now too, though *Wisden* states the pitch was 'certainly not dangerous' the ball was liable to lift at the Nursery End. India chose to bat first, but the pitch suited bowlers, and it was a low-scoring match.

Statham bowled an inswinger on a good length to Contractor, but the ball lifted and hit the batsman in the ribs. He fell to the ground, but after treatment and a drink out in the middle he continued his innings. At lunch a doctor suspected rib damage but the batsman batted on in all for four and a quarter hours, using a runner only after tea. He had in fact cracked a seventh rib; yet he scored 81, half his team's total. Later, he came in at number-eight in the second innings, suitably strapped; subsequently, he was out of the touring team for a month.

England won this match easily in the end, though when Statham went out to bat they were 100 for 7 in reply to India's 168. The bowler proceeded to make his highest Test score, 38 in 80 minutes, during a stand of 84 with Barrington. Statham's bowling on this occasion brought him five good wickets in the match, including his 150th in Tests. His county colleague Greenhough, the leg-spinner, took 5 for 35 in the first innings; this included a spell of 5 for 12 in 5.1 overs which was his great moment in a brief Test career.

The following Indian fixture was at Old Trafford where the visitors suffered further. In the sunshine, Lancashire scored 400 for 5 declared, which was to lead to Pullar's first Test cap. But next day rain restricted play to just under two and a half hours, starting after tea. In indifferent light, Statham broke through. In his third over an inswinger yorked Apte, and the opening ball of his next over lifted and left Umrigar, who was caught by second slip. Shortly, Roy on the back foot was leg-before to a break-back; but Gaekwad, though playing and missing at Statham, lasted 50 minutes before he was caught behind the wicket. Half the Indian side were out for 37 and the fast bowler had 4 for 25. With the light worsening, Statham was rested and when he returned at 6.55pm, bad light stopped play a few minutes early. The next day, the visitors, though following-on, saved the match comfortably.

For the Leeds Test on 2 July, Statham, because of a foot injury, was replaced by Harold Rhodes of Derbyshire. Alan Moss also played, as he had in the previous two Tests.

But Statham missed only one Championship match and then appeared at Old Trafford against Nottinghamshire. Washbrook put the opposition in on a green and lively pitch; Statham's second ball moved away from the left-handed Norman Hill who was thus caught by the wicketkeeper. In his third over, he hit Winfield's leg stump with a break-back. Statham then had Millman and Reg Simpson in difficulty by virtue of great pace and varied movement; and the ball tended to lift even from only just short of a length. The *Manchester Guardian* reported that the way Statham missed the stumps by coats of paint had to be seen to be believed.

He and Higgs bowled a lengthy opening spell in the hot weather, though they did have the benefit of a drink. They limited Simpson to six runs in an hour, which included four for a snick through the slips. At lunch Notts had reached 71 for 2, but straight afterwards the England bowler's luck changed and he had Millman well caught at first slip and Simpson taken at second. This gave him 4 for 23 out of the visitors' 84 for 4. After tea, he returned and had Springall caught in the gully off the old ball and Poole caught off the new.

By also having two tail-enders caught, Statham finished with 24.5-7-44-8, his second-best analysis up to that date, behind his feat at Coventry. His county went on to win the match with ten minutes to spare, although he had to retire during the Notts second innings with a leg strain. This kept him out of the game for three weeks, which included the Manchester Test. For this, Rhodes was selected again, but perhaps because he bowled too short in this Test, and surely because of controversy about his action, it was his last England cap.

Statham was fit again for August, though he was soon on the receiving end of the fastest century of the season; Jim Parks of Sussex was scoring so freely that Statham (as recorded by John Marshall in his book *Old Trafford*) said to him:

"I reckon you can easily get the quickest 100 of the season." To which Parks replied:

"I certainly can't with you bowling." But he did it, in 61 minutes! I should add that Statham was relatively economical with 23-4-58-0.

Statham was able to return for the Test at The Oval, and finished top of the England bowling averages with 17 wickets at 13.11 each (Trueman took 24 wickets at 16.70).

As for the top of the England batting averages, I will content myself with pointing out that M.J.K.Smith averaged 69 and that Statham's innings were 29 not out, 38 and 3 not out!

On 26 August Kent visited Old Trafford and Statham had a score to settle for his poor analysis at Gravesend. The pitch was hard and fast and he bowled Wilson with the first ball of his second over. In his sixth over he had the sweet revenge of having Cowdrey caught behind the wicket for a single and Pettiford leg-before. This gave him 3 for 8, and he later uprooted Jones's leg stump and had Catt taken at fine leg to finish with 5 for 31 out of Kent's 83 all out.

In mid-afternoon, with Lancashire 41 for 3, Washbrook came out to bat. He was applauded all the way to the wicket — it was his last home appearance for the county. He made 50 in this farewell innings, and Statham followed with 44 (2 sixes) to help Lancashire to a useful lead, so that they went on to win inside two days.

Washbrook was taking the opportunity to retire at the age of 44 — he had already stayed on more for Lancashire's benefit than his own. The captaincy of a young side (only Wharton and Grieves of the regulars in 1959 were over 30) was becoming an increasingly difficult task for him; indeed, that was the sort of task it was to be for the next few captains yet.

John Kay wrote of Cyril Washbrook that he "never gave anything but his best in the cause of Lancashire cricket. No man can give more." Statham's opinion was that Washbrook as captain did "a pretty good job, for we were always near the top without getting there."

In this, his last season, the captain took the county to fifth in the table; it was a talented team; and Washbrook over the years had played his part in developing its talents.

Wisden points out that Higgs' continued progress was of great benefit to Statham, who ended this sunny season top of the Lancashire averages with 115 wickets in all matches at 15.65 each. He also topped the national averages, for the second time (if one counts 1954); he had taken 139 wickets at 15.01 each, and in spite of being injured for several weeks he had never bowled quite so many overs in a season (977).

In such hot weather, he had certainly earned his pre-eminence.

Senior Professional in the Caribbean

THE MCC team left Avonmouth on 8 December 1959 on the banana boat *Camito* for the West Indies. They arrived, after some rough weather, about ten days later in Bridgetown.

Statham's colleagues as fast bowlers were Trueman and Moss; the Lancashire bowler himself was the senior professional and a member of the selection committee during the tour. E.W.Swanton wrote: "It is particularly pleasing to see Brian Statham in a position of authority, for the new men could have no better model."

The first major fixture was against Barbados, and the local team proved very strong on a perfect pitch. The last day of the match, 2 January, was unlucky for Statham. He and Trueman had to bowl during the extra half-hour, when Barbados began their second innings needing 58 to win in 28 minutes, Conrad Hunte and Cammie Smith being the batsmen.

In the second over, a brief rainstorm burst, but May neither appealed nor wasted time, much to the crowd's appreciation. But Statham was soon to slip and fall in the act of delivery, after which he bowled off a short run. That over cost 19 runs, including four successive fours by Smith, and the 50 came up in under five overs, so that the batsmen cantered home in 25 minutes. Not only did Statham have an analysis of 3.2-0-38-0, but also his fall had strained a hamstring and he was unfit to play in the First Test a few days later.

This Test, also on a perfect Bridgetown pitch, was a high-scoring draw. For the Second Test at Port of Spain, Trinidad, on 28 January, Statham replaced Moss and on a true, grassless surface England opened with 382. Wes Hall was warned on the first morning for bowling too many bouncers and his partner, Chester Watson, similarly on the second morning.

Statham, and especially Trueman, answered in kind during the last half-hour of the second day, when Hunte and Solomon scored

22 without loss, but there was no more bouncer trouble during the match.

On the Saturday nearly 30,000 people, a record for a match in the West Indies, witnessed the most crucial play of the series. Statham and Trueman were at the centre of it, showing between them nearly all the skills of fast bowling. They did not intimidate the batsmen: Statham produced a bouncer every six overs, roughly speaking, and Trueman did so about every two overs.

Swanton said of Statham: "All day he was beating his man off the pitch, either by the pace at which the ball skidded through or with deviation each way," and John Arlott wrote: "Statham employed the flawless hammering accuracy of his greatness."

Trueman bowled at least as well as his partner, indeed he had the better figures, though no one could regard their success as other than a combined effort. Arlott called it the finest joint operation the pair had yet carried out. And at the time, the comment was made of both bowlers that they seemed to have become five years younger during the morning.

Apart from this fine bowling, I can only find the following reasons for this, the solitary collapse of the West Indian batting in the series. John Arlott states that there was "a hint of sap in the wicket and of humidity in the air"; two important catches had an element of luck about them; and there were two run-outs.

Statham, upwind, and Trueman bowled almost throughout the pre-lunch period. Without addition to the overnight score, Hunte snicked a ball from Statham on to possibly both his boot and his pad, and Trueman, fielding round the corner, took the catch high and one-handed. Nine runs later, Trueman dismissed Kanhai and Sobers in the same over, the latter being caught at first slip after May at third slip had parried a fierce slash: 31 for 3. Just before lunch, Solomon, having been beaten regularly by Statham, was run out, and Worrell was caught off Trueman: 45 for 5 at the interval. Trueman's figures then were 3 for 12, his partner's 1 for 20.

Half an hour after lunch, the fast men were relieved, and Butcher and Alexander added in all 28 in 103 minutes before Statham, who had just returned and had Butcher missed at short leg, trapped the same batsman leg-before: 73 for 6.

Just after tea, the captain, Alexander, fell to Trueman and at 98 for 7 at about 4.15pm, Ramadhin tried to steal a single and the local Test debutant, Charran Singh, was run out by Dexter. And thereby hangs a tale.

That tale is well-documented. Before I mention it, here are the bowling analyses at that stage when the score was 98 for 8: Trueman 19-10-32-4, Statham 18-8-31-2.

The tale is about a riot. Various motives combined to produce a hail of bottles from a section of the overcrowded ringside. The run-out had been the last straw, even though the batsman agreed he was out. The crowd spilled over the ground, and Statham recalls that "ten English players were clustered around one set of stumps, while at the other end stood only myself and the umpire who had given the run-out decision that sparked off the row. The umpire was white and trembling, which was understandable, and my hand was resting lightly on top of the stumps, which was also understandable."

May led the team — it seems that Trueman and Statham with a stump apiece guarded its flanks — back to the pavilion, and the police escorted the umpires. Play was abandoned for the day, mainly owing to broken glass, and later it was announced that the lost time would be made up on subsequent days.

On the Monday morning, the two fast bowlers took another wicket each, so that Trueman finished with 5 for 35 and Statham 3 for 42 of the West Indies' 112 all out. The other two victims had been run out. This innings was, as I have hinted, an exceptionally low total; the next lowest West Indian first innings in this series was 338 for 8 declared. So the 112 all out, as it transpired, was fatal to the home side's hopes in the rubber. May did not enforce the follow-on, but the West Indies needed a near-impossible target in their second innings.

The wickets this time were shared between five England bowlers, but Statham produced two notable overs just before lunch on the last day, at which moment England required seven more wickets. His first ball of the spell kept low and moved in to Worrell, who was leg-before for a duck. Butcher, admittedly needing a runner because of a foot injury, came out and faced Statham's next 11 balls.

Between seven and ten of these 11 balls were said to have beaten the batsman, but he survived them all. The *Guardian* reported that Butcher 'almost turned Statham's first delivery into his stumps, played and missed at the second, which moved away from him and played and missed four times during Statham's next over before opening his score, with a lucky four over the heads of the short legs'. After lunch, only on Statham's third lbw appeal was Butcher sent on his way.

England won the match at about teatime with an hour and three-quarters to spare. The only remaining item I should mention is Ian Peebles' opinion of Statham in this Test: "he gave an exhibition of seam bowling with a worn ball I have seldom seen equalled." I should perhaps add here, for the sake of balance, that the same expert said of Trueman that he "bowled splendidly throughout the trip and, day in, day out, was the spearhead."

The Third Test started a fortnight later, at Kingston, Jamaica, and England scored 277 thanks to opener Cowdrey, who wore improvised padding to counteract the exceptional pace and aggression of Hall and Watson.

The West Indies went in at 2.30pm on the second day. The pitch favoured batsmen as usual; *Wisden* said of this tour that rolling could give the shaven pitches 'such a high polish that sometimes the reflections of batsmen could easily be seen'.

Statham, in his third over, had Hunte caught at short leg and after tea, in his 14th consecutive over, bowled only about his second bouncer. Sobers pulled the ball close to Allen at mid wicket, who reached for the catch but could not hold it, and three runs were scored. The batsman, on two at that time, went on to make 147. Although Statham had beaten opener McMorris repeatedly, the latter was 31 not out of his team's 81 for 2 made in two hours 35 minutes that day.

On the third morning, Statham fell in delivering his second ball, which was perhaps a bad omen in that no wicket was captured all that day. At lunch, McMorris, having added nine in 90 minutes, compared to Sobers' 53, had made 40 in 245 minutes.

The new ball was taken at 178 for 2 in mid-afternoon and at 189 for 2 Statham was bowling his third over with it. McMorris, 65 in five and a half hours, was facing. A short ball hit the batsman in the chest, but after getting his breath back McMorris was able to face the last ball of the over. However, he was spitting blood, and after a doctor had come on to the field with the West Indian captain, the batsman was led back to the pavilion. He was taken for an X-ray, which showed bad bruising of the lung. It was announced that he would continue batting on the next day, but only if required.

Colin Cowdrey, while explaining the usefulness of a bouncer against a batsman who is coming forward even before the ball has left the bowler's hand, illuminates this incident in his autobiography:

> "I have a very clear recollection of Easton McMorris keeping Brian Statham at bay effectively by thrusting out his front foot down the line. Brian Statham, a magnificent competitor yet the fairest sportsman in all the world, warned him quietly and courteously that if he continued in this vein he would be given one or two nasty bouncers. I have never known a warning being given like that before or since; I cannot envisage it happening in today's [1] game. Unhappily, McMorris did not heed the warning and two overs later walked straight into a short-pitched delivery which hit him a severe blow under the heart. He was seriously hurt and had to be taken to hospital. No one was more upset about it than Brian Statham, but McMorris was taking advantage of his good nature and at the end of the match, when he had fully recovered, he was big enough to admit that no blame could be laid at Brian Statham's door."

The West Indies finished that day at 291 for 2 but England came back the next day, before a record Jamaican crowd. Immediately after lunch the home team went from 329 for 3 to 329 for 6, whereupon McMorris, with his chest protected, returned briefly; West Indies were all out with a lead, after all, of only 76. Cowdrey followed with an innings which he calls "the best I have ever played" and England had a lead of 204 with a day to go when Statham joined Allen.

If this last-wicket pair had been separated at once on the final morning, the West Indians would have needed 205 in 290 minutes; but the pair stayed 45 minutes, scoring 25, so that the target had become 230 in 245 minutes. The pitch was at last showing signs of cracking, which was an element now in England's favour.

With McMorris opening again, the West Indies responded in an

[1]Written in 1976.

exciting finish with 175 for 6, four of whom were bowled by Trueman, who thus saved the match for England. Statham had trouble in this innings with his left foot, completing his first over from a short run. Sore toes and a bad blister were the trouble; it seems that the boot with the toe-cap cut out, which had previously benefited him in Australia, again solved the problem. With the adapted boot, he was able to continue, though John Arlott called it brave.

So England retained their 1-0 lead. Statham and Trueman were duly rested for the next game, against the Leeward Islands, and they were able to relax over tea with Sir Anthony and Lady Eden at the politician's holiday home in Antigua. However, though Statham's foot recovered by being rested for this match and the next, the bowler received a set-back of a different sort just before the Fourth Test.

The news reached him from England that his five and a half-year-old elder son Terence was seriously ill. Terence had gone into hospital to have his tonsils out on about 28 February, but the real problem arose when he was back at home. On about 8 March Mrs Statham found her son with his head on his shoulder and unable to lift it.

The Old Trafford physiotherapist and a specialist saw the boy. Belatedly, it was now realized that he had been incubating chicken-pox at the time of the tonsil operation. He was taken to hospital near Manchester, and his neck was put into a collar.

On 9 March Statham played in the Fourth Test at Georgetown, knowing that his son was ill. Probably referring to the second day's play, the bowler recalls:

"I had finished my over and was moving to my position on the edge of the boundary when a spectator getting a free show of the match, sprawled full length on a branch of a tree overhanging the ground, shouted down: 'Hey, Statham, man. Your son is dead!' "

He continues: "I froze at the shock of the news. At the tea interval I had checked and there had been no further message from England on Terence's condition. But this spectator had his radio and I wondered if he had picked up a news flash from England. I sent an anxious enquiry to the pavilion but no one had heard anything."

However, only when he spoke on the phone to his wife that

evening, was he sure that his son was alive. The *Manchester Evening News* of 10 March reported Mrs Statham as saying that Terence was over the worst of it and had just begun to improve.

Although the MCC team manager, Walter Robins, told Statham he could return home whenever he wished, the bowler stayed for the duration of the Test. He 'phoned England daily, and then flew home the day after the match ended. Terence benefited from his father's arrival back home, and was soon recovering.

Statham, in his book *Flying Bails,* publicly thanked both MCC and the West Indian Board of Control for their generosity with the arrangements.

Strangely, three days later, Peter May also had to fly home early. This was on medical advice, because of a continually reopening operation wound.

Cowdrey captained England in two high-scoring draws, at Georgetown and in the final Test, so a series went England's way for the first time in their five tours to the Caribbean.

Trueman had taken over as senior professional, which for him set the seal on a successful tour. He finished with the most wickets and the best bowling average, whether one looked at the Tests or at all first-class matches.

Finally, *Wisden* said of Statham's part: 'Perhaps more than any other bowler in the series he beat the bat, no mean feat on such pitches, without reward'. In the end, though, I doubt whether the bowler himself recalled things that way. Terence's recovery, and England's victory, were reward enough by then.

10.66 And All That

THE sunny weather of 1959 was not likely to repeat itself in the following summer. It did not; rain affected many matches in 1960.

Washbrook's successor as Lancashire's captain was R.W.(Bob) Barber, an amateur, and in a throwback to earlier years he was given the traditional status of his post. He was even booked in at hotels separate from the team's hotels. He had a difficult reign. In retrospect, he was probably appointed too early in his career. Nevertheless, Lancashire did very well in the 1960 Championship.

Statham's most successful match was at Grace Road, Leicester, starting on 21 May. When the players arrived, they could see that a bowler's match was in prospect. Because the ground was then shared with the local education authority, the marks of a recent athletics meeting were visible; moreover, the pitch was damp and the light was poor.

Thus *The Guardian's* Eric Todd reported that the winner of the toss, home captain Willie Watson, "having learned that Statham was alive and well, retired for private meditation before throwing his opponents to the lions, as it were." Todd felt that conditions were slightly farcical and this may have contributed to the humour with which he reports this match. He continued with: "Mischief was early afoot and Pullar, having saved his teeth, lost his other stumps to a ball which came through at ankle height."

Lancashire totalled 138, all the wickets falling to the opening fast bowlers. The above reporter said the ball was doing everything except boomerang.

In such circumstances, Statham and Colin Hilton now dismissed Leicestershire for only 37, the top score being seven. Harold Bird retired hurt and went to hospital, said Eric Todd, "to have his knuckles counted." Bird had severe bruising but recovered for the next fixture. Statham bowled three men, had three caught by the 'keeper and one at slip, for an analysis of 10-2-17-7. Hilton backed him up splendidly, was sometimes faster than his partner, and 'softened up' the batsmen.

On the Monday, the pitch had dried out and few deliveries behaved abnormally. Leicester soon began their second innings, needing 226 to win. They began hopefully — the 50 was reached without mishap in under an hour, and Hilton had lost his previous accuracy. But then the surface seemed to liven up and Watson was hit four times on the body before Statham uprooted the left-hander's off stump. Next, Hallam was forced back so far by the England bowler that he hit his wicket as well as playing the ball on: 68 for 2, last man 41.

Statham, in his first over after lunch, removed Gardner's off stump. And he bowled Cromack for a duck, so that he had, without the aid of the fielders, dismissed four players for two runs during this purple patch. When he also bowled Pratt, he had taken all the first five wickets.

Then Greenhough bowled two men before Statham bowled the last two. Leicester were 103 all out (Bird was absent hurt), Lancashire being easy winners. Eric Todd described Statham as "removing stumps with strict impartiality." If one counts Hallam as effectively bowled, Statham had bowled out all his seven victims. His analysis was 18.4-7-41-7: 14 wickets in the match for 58, at the time second only to his Coventry match haul.

Let the final comment on the game rest with *The Guardian* reporter. He said that the Lancashire driver drew his coach up outside the Leicester dressing-room at three o'clock, and that by 3.45pm the contest was all over — so the home team had taken the hint.

Statham, after a useful contribution to a narrow victory over Warwickshire, next made himself unpopular with the Worcestershire batsmen. On the first morning, at Worcester, he met success early. The fixture was for George Dews' Benefit but after quarter of an hour's play it was hardly living up to its title. Dews, though batting at number-five, was already walking out to the middle — with only four runs on the board, and to face a fast bowler who had just taken three wickets in four balls. To Dews' credit, he went on to score 27 of his team's 82 all out.

By the end of that innings, Statham, in eight days of late May, had taken 27 wickets for 169 runs. It was, of course, a victorious time for Lancashire.

During this season of 1960 the South Africans visited England; they lost the First Test by 100 runs and on 25 June went to the

Lord's Test. *Wisden* states: 'To avoid the possibility of the supposed ridge near a length at one end interfering with the game, the pitch was moved a yard nearer the pavilion'. *The Guardian* reported that this was a big improvement and that playing forward was safe almost throughout the Test.

Interrupted by rain, England scored 362 for 8 by Friday evening. A declaration led to McGlew and Goddard coming to the wicket when play began on the Saturday, during which the crowd reached 27,000. The above-quoted newspaper said that this day belonged almost entirely to Statham, who for three and three-quarter hours (during which he bowled 27 of the 31 overs which England bowled from the Pavilion end) gave an 'object lesson to Adcock and Griffin on how to bowl fast through a humid atmosphere and on a wicket still green enough to help movement off the seam'.

The report added that Statham did all the two South African bowlers had failed to do — he pitched up (unlike Adcock), and he bowled straight (unlike Griffin). He made the batsmen play at nearly every ball. His deliveries could swing either way, or break either way and he varied his pace subtly. The crowd was fascinated.

The South Africans were no match for Statham on the day. He took in total 7 for 71, and yet *The Times* report still claimed that 'most batsmen would agree that now D.V.P.Wright has retired Statham is the world's unluckiest bowler'. I think this comment was prompted by the reporter's remark that Statham only conceded about 15 runs in front of the wicket. This distribution, coupled with the fact that there was generally no third man or long leg, suggests there were quite a few snicks for four — indeed, there were two in his first over.

Statham was admirably supported by Moss, although Trueman, hindered by twisting an ankle in Adcock's footholds, had difficulty finding his length.

Under a lowering sky, Statham bowled the first ball of the innings. It was of good length, lifted and moved away, flying off the shoulder of McGlew's bat high over gully. Half an hour later, Statham produced a ball to the left-handed Goddard which pitched on the leg stump, moved 'down the slope' (towards the Tavern), and sent the off stump cartwheeling.

At 12.30pm McGlew, on the back foot which Hutton, in retrospect, commented was a risky move throughout this match, was leg-before to a ball from Statham which kept low and came in. Moss dismissed O'Linn before the Lancashire bowler had Waite (who in the previous two balls had been hit on the finger and had given a half-chance) caught off an outswinger: 69 for 4.

McLean hooked Statham powerfully twice. Then came a tempting outswinger, just short of a length. McLean cut it hard, with the full face of the bat. Cowdrey, at second slip, nonchalantly caught it as if he was wearing Parks' gloves, the ball bruising his chest.

Wesley turned his first ball from Statham knee-high to Trueman in the leg trap, but the chance went down. Soon afterwards, Statham was rested after 100 minutes' bowling for figures of 12-5-36-4. Even the South African batsmen applauded him. Len Hutton reported that he had seen only one loose ball in the spell.

After lunch (taken at 88 for 6), there was a hint of sunshine, and the tail-enders fought hard. Statham had returned and soon had Wesley caught off an outswinger, but runs were coming steadily. Griffin lofted Statham over mid on, the only driven four which the bowler conceded in the day; but removal of the leg stump was the revenge. When South Africa were all out for 152, Statham's analysis was 20-5-63-6; Moss had taken 4 for 35.

The follow-on began at about 3.30pm and when a thunderstorm stopped play at 5pm, South Africa were 34 for the loss of McGlew, whom Statham had forced to chop an inswinger on to his stumps.

After a well-earned Sunday rest, Statham was back at 11 o'clock on the Monday. It was damp and overcast, but the crowd built up to 15,000. The Queen was due to visit Lord's at teatime. When the score was 49 Statham took two wickets: Goddard snicked a ball to the 'keeper, and Waite was leg-before to one which came in. Trueman, Moss and Dexter reduced the South Africans to 132 for 8 at lunch, and by 2.25pm Statham had completed England's innings victory by bowling the last two men. In dismissing Griffin, he broke the top of the middle stump.

Statham's analysis was 21-6-34-5, which gave him 11 for 97 in the match. One had to go back to Bill Voce in 1929-30 to find an England fast bowler taking 11 wickets in a Test.

Statham wrote later: "Really, I should never have had the chance. I bowled 41 overs in that game, bowling almost throughout both South African innings. I was whacked long before the finish and Colin Cowdrey might have done better in insisting that I bowled in shorter spells. It was as much my fault as his. Every time he asked me if I was happy to go on I said 'okay'. I was never the same force again that summer."

Still, he won two crates of sherry for his figures in the two innings!

Ten days later, the Third Test started at Nottingham and England won the match and thus the series. By the Friday evening South Africa had replied to England's 287 with 88 and 34 for 3. The next morning McGlew, in particular, played well and the crowd were impressed by the visitors' recovery to 91 for 3. But at that score an unfortunate incident occurred, involving Statham as a fielder.

Moss bowled over the wicket to the left-handed O'Linn. The batsman pushed the ball towards Statham at extra cover. Moss moved to his right with a view to fielding the ball, but in so doing he collided with McGlew, who had been called for a quick single. Moreover, O'Linn was also running up the same side of the pitch.

Statham concentrated only on the ball, which he picked up, and threw at the striker's stumps, scoring a direct hit. McGlew, who had continued his interrupted course, was short of safety by a yard or even two.

England's appeal was upheld by the square-leg umpire. But the crowd thought this was unfair on McGlew and voiced their disapproval. England's captain, Cowdrey, tried to bring the batsman back. The umpires, however, correctly told him that the die was cast, and a legal dismissal had occurred. As Statham points out, Moss had not deliberately hindered McGlew. Cowdrey nevertheless wrote later: "What I should have done, as experience has now taught me, was to have withdrawn the appeal."

Although South Africa continued the fight-back, England by close of play had virtually won the match. With the two following Tests being drawn, the rubber went England's way by 3-0.

By then, Statham and Trueman had bowled together in every Test of a series for the first of only two times and they had taken 52 wickets between them of the England bowlers' 79. The Lancashire player had taken 27 wickets (his best for any one series) at 18.18 each. Incidentally, although Statham regarded McGlew as his 'bunny', he dismissed the other opener, Goddard, nine times in 11 meetings (disregarding a run-out) in all matches on this tour.

Away from the Test scene, on 13 July Statham was honoured

with the captaincy of the Players against the Gentlemen at Lord's. In the Championship table, one finds Lancashire at the top for three days from 26 July, with Yorkshire second. By 30 July the positions were reversed. This date was the first day of the Roses match at Old Trafford, for which Statham returned after missing the preceding fixture because of throat trouble. The game was also the joint Benefit match of Malcolm Hilton and Tattersall, although neither was actually playing.

The Saturday crowd was only a few thousand when play began — but the match's importance was not to be denied, and by just after lunch the attendance had grown to over 20,000. Yorkshire batted first and Statham's opening spell of 8-1-19-0 was reported as being disappointing and perhaps reflecting his recent illness.

The pitch was true, but by virtue of bowling a full length Higgs and, later, his England partner, did meet with success — especially after the wicket was freshened by rain at three o'clock. When half the Yorkshire side were out for 113, Statham had contributed the dismissals, leg-before, of Sharpe and Illingworth. The latter was his 100th wicket of the season. Then, encouraged by the effect of the shower, he bowled Close for 63 with an inswinger, had Don Wilson lbw and yorked Vic Wilson. When Yorkshire were all out for 154, Statham had the much-improved analysis of 23-7-43-5, and Higgs had taken 4 for 48.

On Bank Holiday Monday, Lancashire took their total past their opponents' with only one wicket down. But then rain stopped play for two hours and so affected the pitch that after tea Lancashire went from 187 for 3 to 226 all out. The lead gave them two points but a further two were missed because Yorkshire had scored the faster.

When the visitors went in towards 6 o'clock, an hour's drying and then the roller had cured the pitch of its nasty lift. However, Statham sent the near-30,000 crowd home in a happier mood because he had Stott caught off a mis-hook and Padgett lbw to a break-back: 19 for 2 at the close.

On the last morning, Statham opened with six overs for one run and then he had Close leg-before to a ball which nipped into him. Higgs had already bowled Ken Taylor and the night-watchman Binks, so half the side were out for 36 and Yorkshire were still 36 behind! Statham was rested after a spell of 1 for 4 in ten overs.

At lunch the score was 107 for 7, mainly thanks to Sharpe, whom Statham later had leg-before for 46 as Yorkshire totalled 149. The England bowler's analysis was 24-13-23-4. Don Wilson's 32 not out had given Yorkshire a slim chance because Lancashire needed 78 in two hours.

Vic Wilson at once set a defensive field; after an hour, the score was 26 for 1. Chasing runs began to invite trouble: 32 for 3 after 75 minutes. Then Trueman yorked Marner, and after Grieves and Collins had nudged 11 in ten minutes, the latter and then Statham were both out trying to force Ryan: 43 for 6. With 10 or 12 points and top place in the table at stake, Lancashire thus needed 35 runs in the last half-hour, while Yorkshire needed four wickets. A draw would benefit Yorkshire (top) more than it would Lancashire (second).

In the final two overs, 16 runs were wanted. Ryan bowled the penultimate over and although ten runs came (Clayton hit two brave fours) Grieves was caught off the last ball: 72 for 7, last man 27. So off the last over, from Trueman, six were needed to win.

Clayton drove the first ball for a single, Greenhough was bowled by the second. Dyson scrambled two leg byes off the third and then a single off the fourth, even though he had merely stopped the latter in his blockhole.

The penultimate ball was edged by Clayton for a single: 77 for 8 and the teams were level. Lancashire wanted one run to win off the last ball of the match, from Trueman to Dyson. It was very fast. To the home supporters, Dyson leg-glanced it; to the Yorkshire supporters, he snicked it via his pad. Anyway, the ball raced down to the fine-leg boundary, and Lancashire had won. Statham counted this match among the best he played in.

The very next day, the new Championship leaders met Gloucestershire at Bristol. The pitch favoured fast bowling — the ball moved off the seam and it tended to keep low. Lancashire batted first and were a mere 62 for 8 when Statham went out to bat; he was applauded generously. But as *The Guardian* pointed out, little did the locals suspect that the score would be doubled before Statham returned! Batting discreetly, he helped Collins to add 44; and during a last-wicket stand with Higgs he opened out, driving Allen over long on for six. His 34 not out was the top score in the innings of 125 all out.

In mid-afternoon, the home team went in. Their first wicket fell at 28, Statham having Young caught at first slip. Then the England bowler broke through. Nicholls, beaten for the third successive ball, was leg-before, and when the score was 50, Statham took three more wickets for no runs. He had Tom Graveney lbw to a ball which came in; he bowled Mortimore first ball; and, after Pugh had swished at the hat-trick ball, he bowled him immediately afterwards.

Statham had taken the first five wickets and when Higgs dismissed Carpenter, Gloucester were 50 for 6. The England bowler later had Allen leg-before, after which he was rested with figures of 6 for 39 off 20 overs in all.

Gloucester, 122 for 9 overnight, were all out for 123 — two runs behind Lancashire — next morning, when Statham removed the last man's off stump to finish with 7 for 50. As in the Yorkshire match, the lead brought Lancashire only two points not four; but they went on to a narrow victory and stayed top of the table, even though Yorkshire simultaneously won.

But the leadership changed hands on 16 August. And it did so permanently. On that day Lancashire lost to Essex at Southend while Yorkshire won again. Including these two games, but excluding 'no decision' matches (Yorkshire had two such, Lancashire had one), the respective points won in their last five fixtures were 56 by Yorkshire and 8 by Lancashire. So no one could dispute Yorkshire's right to the title.

But if his team had to be satisfied with second place, Statham himself did not. He topped the national averages for the second successive year and no fast bowler had done that since Larwood was top of the list in 1931 and 1932.

Although, mainly because of the Tests, Statham missed 13 Championship games, he took 106 wickets for Lancashire in all matches for only 10.66 runs each. This is the cheapest 100 wickets in a season ever taken for the county. It was probably the biggest individual contribution to Lancashire's finishing as high as second; and their *Wisden* correspondent reported: 'By far the most pleasing feature of the summer was the continued wonderful form of Statham'.

Just after the end of the 1960 season, Statham and several England colleagues flew out to Southern Africa for a month. This was a private tour arranged by Ron Roberts, a cricket journalist, writer and inveterate traveller. The Anglo-Australian team he gathered was known as a Commonwealth XI or 'The Cavaliers'. The Lancashire bowler had the rare experience for him of playing under Benaud's captaincy, which favourably impressed him. Statham, in his four matches, all Cavalier wins, took 21 wickets.

Benefit Season

STATHAM, after 11 seasons during which he had taken in total over 1,000 wickets for his county, was granted a benefit year in 1961. He was given the Lancashire versus Australians match and he wrote: "No professional could ask for a finer gesture than that." Luckily, too, the summer was mainly fine.

But it was not to be an outstanding season for Statham (his 100 first-class wickets cost him 20 runs each), for Lancashire (who slumped to 13th), or for England (beaten 2-1 by Australia). Statham bowled over a thousand overs in a first-class season for the only time, but he had to put up with many slow pitches and poor Lancashire slip-catching. Higgs and big Colin Hilton supported him well, if without distinction.

Statham's best county match was at the end of May against Hampshire. On the first day, the close-cropped Old Trafford pitch was expected to help the batsmen, but Statham, with good support from the other two pace men, put Lancashire on top. He knocked back Gray's off stump for a single, and though Roy Marshall typically hit two early fours, the West Indian was leg-before to Statham at ten. When Hampshire came in to lunch at 90 for 3, the England bowler had also claimed the other wicket by removing Livingstone's off bail.

Just after the interval Statham had Sainsbury caught and he bowled Baldry, for figures of 5 for 23 of the visitors' 91 for 5. Later he finished the innings of 152 by bowling White for an analysis of 23-12-27-6, and Lancashire went on to win the match, thanks mainly to their pace bowlers.

Regarding the Ashes series, Statham played in four Tests, being injured for the other. The draw at Edgbaston was a batsman's match. The Second Test at Lord's on 22 June, however, took place on a bowler's pitch. When dismissing McDonald, Statham took his 200th Test wicket, a milestone previously reached only by Grimmett, Bedser, Lindwall and Benaud. But Australia in this Test conceded little else to any England player, and at 12.45pm on the fourth day they found themselves needing only 69 to win.

Yet, encouraged by the pitch, by the cloudy, humid conditions and by the 'umbrella' field, Statham and Trueman put England in with a chance. McDonald began with 14 out of 15 in as many minutes, but then Trueman had him well caught in the gully. In the next over, Statham produced a bumper off which Lawry, hooking, was caught by the 'keeper. Next, O'Neill tried to play a fast, full-length ball from Statham off the back foot and his off stump was sent flying. When Harvey fell to Trueman, Australia were 19 for 4 after eight hostile overs.

But Simpson and Burge, helped by fours snicked past the close field, took the score to 35 before Statham bowled the last ball before lunch. It was a straight bouncer which Burge mis-hooked off the splice up towards the square-leg umpire. Lock, from leg slip, ran about eight yards and dived for the catch but could only get his fingertips to it. After lunch, Australia did not look back. Although Statham had Simpson caught in the gully off a lifter at 58, he finally suffered two leg side fours from Burge, who thus gave Australia victory.

Immediately after the match, the pitch was surveyed. The wicket for the 1960 Lord's Test had been moved towards the Pavilion to avoid the supposed ridge, but now it had again been located normally. The result, despite the heavy roller, was regarded by *The Times* as a 'wretched wicket'. Benaud, among others, denounced the ridge and certainly the bounce was uneven.

After the survey, MCC announced that there were slight depressions and high points and that one of the latter may have affected the bounce at the Nursery End. Relaying of the turf in time for the next season was promised and subsequently carried out.

A few days later, on Saturday, 1 July, Statham's Benefit match against the tourists began. *The Guardian* of that day carried an article on the beneficiary by Eric Todd, who wrote of Statham's bowling: "For every wicket he has taken he has lost two through dropped catches; for every successful appeal — and he never makes one idly — he has had two rejected; and hundreds of stumps and bails have felt the wind rather than the impact of his delivery."

And of his character: "Off the field he is not an outstanding conversationalist and chooses his company shrewdly. He prefers to rest and read, yet he cannot be described as unsociable. He rarely plays cards but he is generous in his advice to those who do, often with peculiar results."

As for the match itself, Statham came out to toss the coin with Benaud, though Barber was actually captain. Lancashire won and chose to bat on a plumb-looking pitch. It turned out to be a batsman's match throughout. As Lancashire amassed a big score, thanks mainly to Pullar and later Clayton, the crowd approached 20,000 on a warm, sunny day. There were 11,746 paying customers, producing £2,305 gate money, half of which would be allocated to Statham. A collection for him realized £302. At the end of the day, he went in to bat and the Australians granted him the traditional single to get off the mark. He scored 16.

On the Monday, which was cloudy and cool, only 3,000 arrrived for the start but this increased to over 10,000 after lunch. The gate money was £1,247 and a collection raised £482. While the tourists speedily approached Lancashire's score of 346, Statham bowled only 15 overs in the day, because Barber could afford, with no Championship points at stake, to aim at keeping Statham fresh for the imminent Third Test.

But, ironically, the bowler now strained his left side, a recurrence of an injury of a couple of weeks earlier, and after tea each ball of his two overs caused him pain. Then rain stopped play in any case. Statham told the county secretary, Geoffrey Howard, to let MCC know, and this led to Les Jackson's inclusion in the Test team in place of the Lancashire player.

The next day, Statham was unable to take the field. The Australians went on to a huge total, but the play was rather academic because a result was so unlikely. Only a few hundred spectators turned up for the start and there were only about 1,000 after lunch, even though the weather brightened. Of the home players, Marner pleased the crowd most by his batting late in the day. A gate of £124 brought the match receipts to £3,676, and the money from the collections finally reached over £800.

These figures, it was reported, assured Statham of over £2,000 from the match, after expenses, and of a grand total from his benefit season of over £10,000. This eventually came to £13,047, at the time the biggest benefit of any cricketer except Washbrook, who in 1948 received £14,000.

Statham was unable to play two days later in the Headingley

Test, in which England levelled the series thanks mainly to Trueman (11 for 88). But he returned for the Old Trafford Test at the end of July. Jackson, despite bowling soundly at Leeds, lost his place, though Flavell was selected as a third fast bowler.

Benaud chose to bat but on a green pitch, with some early moisture, the England bowlers were hostile. The pitch gave them movement and lift, and its pace varied. It was a grey morning but 20,000 people soon arrived. Trueman opened and then Statham, from the City End, fell when about to deliver his second ball. But his fifth ball moved away from Simpson's half-forward stroke and the batsman was caught at the wicket.

Then Lawry and Harvey scored well and after 25 minutes Flavell replaced Statham. After 45 minutes Statham returned for Trueman at the Stretford end, where the wind was more helpful. The Lancashire bowler conceded two singles which took Australia to 51. His third ball left Harvey, and Subba Row in the slips scooped up a superb low catch, which he confirmed to the umpire.

Now O'Neill came in for what Jack Fingleton described as an ordeal. Flavell found lift in the pitch and hit O'Neill's thigh three times, the batsman calling for an extra thigh pad. In half an hour he had scored only a single, when a ball from Statham hit his protector. O'Neill fell down, but was able to continue, though he needed a drink and was slightly sick. His protector had to be hammered back into shape by Dexter.

O'Neill replied to Statham with a boundary but soon he was out when trying to hook a Trueman bumper which broke a blood-vessel in his wrist and made him fall and hit his stumps. Eleven hard-earned runs!

After lunch, Flavell took his first Test wicket but rain stopped play for the day at 124 for 4, with Lawry 64 not out.

The next morning, the 15,000 people who were in the ground when play began, and the 5,000 who soon followed, saw Statham at his best. He bowled for 90 minutes from the Stretford end, while Flavell and Dexter shared the other end. Trueman was held back in case the new ball materialized.

Statham was helped by a breeze and by a pitch which had retained its responsiveness. The last ball of his fourth over, moving in to Lawry a fraction, beat the batsman's half-forward defence and had him leg-before: 150 for 5. In his next over, he beat Booth's bat with three successive balls which moved away. At 12.30pm Mackay glanced a Statham inswinger off the full face of the bat but the deflection was too small and Murray caught it. Ten minutes later Booth turned the same bowler low to short square-leg: 185 for 7, of whom Statham had dismissed five.

Dexter took the last three wickets quickly, so that Australia were all out for 190, having just lost six men for 66 (Statham 3 for 18) with Trueman only looking on! *The Times* said: 'Wonderfully enough, Statham seems to be bowling as well as ever'. His full analysis was 21-3-53-5.

England kept themselves in a strong position by making 367. But this was to be an historic Test; rarely has one match so often proved that it is never won until it is lost. And at stake was a 2-1 lead with only one Test to follow.

On the last morning, Allen's spin reduced Australia from their overnight 331 for 6, a hopeful position, to 334 for 9, the brink of defeat. Their lead then was only 157. But now Davidson hammered Allen out of the firing line, and the England pace bowlers simply could not remove either Davidson, who grabbed most of the strike, or number-11, McKenzie. This last pair added 98. (A consolation for the England bowlers: McKenzie in the previous Sheffield Shield had occasionally opened his State's innings, and had scored well.)

So England were set to make 256 in 230 minutes and Dexter led them to another strong position, 150 for 1 in 125 minutes. Yet, 20 minutes later, at tea, England were 163 for 5. This was the work of Benaud, bowling round the wicket into footmarks, which made up for his painful shoulder tendon in that they allowed him to turn the ball.

At 5.40pm, with 20 minutes to go, Australia won, and thus retained the Ashes. The final victim of this great match was one of its initial heroes: Statham, clean bowled, in front of his own crowd, who had already seen his bowling foiled by Australia's last pair.

A Clouded Summer

STATHAM was not available for MCC's tour of India and Pakistan in 1961-2 (nor were Cowdrey and Trueman). But although *Wisden* is critical of the stay-at-home players, the Lancashire bowler had surely done his stint ten years earlier.

As for the county scene, Lancashire now relieved Barber of the captaincy, and John Kay recalls that there was talk "even of asking Statham to undertake the leadership as well as do the bulk of the bowling." Barber had been seen to dislike the post anyway and also the county felt that his playing ability, especially his bowling, would develop more quickly without the burden of captaincy.

In the event, the new captain was another amateur (in the last year of the distinction) — Joe Blackledge. He was new to first-class cricket but he had met success in the Northern League, had played occasionally for the county Second XI, and was judged to have the right qualities. It was hoped that Grieves, as senior professional, would be able to advise him, but the Australian left to go into business and appeared only for Stockport in 1962. This was the first bad omen; a spate of injuries was another.

In 1962 the weather was poor and so was Lancashire's performance. The county finished next to bottom, their lowest ever, with two wins (each against the Championship leaders of the moment!) out of 32 matches. Statham's wickets, though totalling over a hundred in first-class cricket, cost him more than in any other home season. Even so, his figure of 23.25 was top of Lancashire's Championship averages.

His season had a sad beginning because he was playing at Leicester on 21 May when he heard that his father had died at home near Manchester.

He resumed cricket against the Pakistani tourists, taking 5 for 54 in their first innings of a drawn game at the end of May, but Lancashire and success did not go together in 1962 (except that Bond made over 2,000 runs for the county which no one has done since).

Only once did Statham take as many as six wickets in an innings;

this was in the Roses match at Old Trafford on 4 August, when Yorkshire were challenging for the Championship. The grassy pitch helped Statham and Colin Hilton (who had a better season than Higgs) to bring Yorkshire down to 79 for 6, in front of a crowd building up to over 10,000. The two bowlers soon accounted for the openers, Statham bowling Hampshire with an inswinging yorker. Then a Statham outswinger found Close unable to reach the pitch of the ball, which he snicked to the 'keeper: 42 for 3. When the same bowler hit Illingworth's stumps, Richard Hutton, aged 19, came out to bat on his debut for Yorkshire. He had just won a Cambridge Blue in his first year.

But Statham soon made him play a ball on to his foot, and up into short leg's hands: Yorkshire 57 for 5, Statham having 4 for 21. In the second over after lunch, he yorked Vic Wilson and this brought Trueman in to join Sharpe. Trueman played and missed five times at Statham in two overs, and in ten minutes he touched the ball once, whereupon he doffed his cap to the crowd. Then he lofted Statham for two fours in an over as he went on to score 38.

It is worth noting here that Yorkshire's first innings lead turned out to be only 33, which represented four points to them, and that they won the Championship a month later by only four points! Here's to Trueman's batsmanship!

Sharpe's fine century, mostly scored with the tail-enders, accounted for half his team's runs from the bat. The bowlers could probably have done with a new ball, but the 85th over, the only criterion, was not quite reached. Statham's sixth wicket was Don Wilson and his final analysis was 32-9-68-6. Rain prevented any decision in the match beyond that of first-innings points.

Joe Blackledge suffered a broken finger in this match and, with Barber preferring not to deputize as captain, Statham took over. Indeed, he went on to lead Lancashire for six consecutive matches until Blackledge was able to return.

The Test series became an easy 4-0 win over Pakistan. Statham and Trueman opened in three of the matches, the Lancashire player being replaced by Coldwell at Lord's and The Oval. In the former game, this was due to injury; in the latter it was due to the selectors' desire to blood new players. At The Oval, Trueman also stood down, for Larter. All four bowlers performed creditably in the series, thus satisfying the selectors, who had the coming visit to Australia in view.

Bradman, Bowled Statham

STATHAM was included in the MCC team to tour Australia in 1962-3, Trueman, Coldwell and Larter being his fast-bowling colleagues. The two latter in 1962 had been the leading bowlers of their respective counties, and each had taken nine wickets in his debut Test against Pakistan. With Trueman taking 153 wickets that summer, Statham indeed had had the least impressive season of the quartet.

But his experience, accuracy and reliability were still in demand for such an important tour — especially as the 22-year-old Larter's assets for it were relatively unproven. Of the other fast bowlers who might have been selected, perhaps Flavell, injured, was the unluckiest.

The tour was not a marked success for Statham. *Wisden's* comment on his performance is echoed by Swanton and justified by the bowler's ordinary figures: "although always a willing worker who gave little away, he had lost the zip which previously made him so dangerous." But only Trueman of the four fast bowlers was successful. The series on the whole belonged to the batsmen of both sides and only two Tests produced a result: one win each. Thus Australia retained the Ashes in a disappointing rubber.

Trueman and Statham opened the bowling in all five Tests, for only the second time in any series. Given Australian conditions, Coldwell (two Tests) was a little lacking in speed and Larter (no Tests) in accuracy, according to *Wisden*.

On 26 January, during the drawn Fourth Test at Adelaide, Statham took his 237th Test wicket, which beat Bedser's world record. Davidson and Barry Shepherd, the Western Australia captain, resumed on the second day at 322 for 5 and Trueman opened in a hostile fashion which Shepherd did not enjoy. Statham, in his second over of the morning, bowled a short ball outside the left-handed Shepherd's off stump. But the batsman waved his bat at it and was caught in the gully by Trueman. The England players surrounded Statham with their congratulations. He held the record for only about seven weeks, because Trueman overtook him in New Zealand.

On Wednesday, 6 February, MCC played a one day game for charity, against the Prime Minister's XI at the picturesque Oval at Canberra. Prime Minister Robert Menzies, a great cricket lover, was continuing a traditional fixture he had inaugurated in 1951 against the West Indians. MCC had played his XI in 1954-5 and 1958-9 but for Statham this 1962-3 game was his first.

And it was more of an occasion than usual because Sir Donald Bradman was to play alongside first-class cricketers for the first time since a 1948-9 Sheffield Shield match.

So now 10,000 people, a ground record, producing £1,600 for charity, were attracted, and they spread on to the surrounding banks. The weather was sunny and the atmosphere was likened to that of a garden party. The spectators included not only Mr Menzies (whom the Queen knighted during the next month), but Viscount de L'Isle (the Governor-General and another cricket enthusiast), and, of course, the Duke of Norfolk who was the MCC tour manager.

Informality was the order of the day: MCC batted first by arrangement, and the intervals were as long as suited — lunch was 50 minutes. On a good pitch, the tourists scored rapidly — Bradman was probably happy to be at slip! David Sheppard made 72 at a run-a-minute, and after lunch MCC added 105 in 45 minutes. Cowdrey and Knight hit many boundaries, indeed Knight hit 6 fours in nine balls from Benaud, but the only six was credited to Trueman.

Thus the visitors totalled 253 in 160 minutes, and the Prime Minister's XI replied with 101 for 2 in under an hour before tea, Cowper scoring freely off Trueman and Bedser. The latter's real function was assistant tour manager, but he was still looking fit and had played a useful part in MCC net practices.

Ten minutes after tea, Bradman came out to bat at number-five. He was applauded all the way to the wicket by the crowd and by the fielding side. He was now aged 54 and chairman of the Australian Board of Control, but he too looked fit and everyone was hoping he would make runs. He had not neglected to practise for the match.

Graveney was to bowl the first ball to Bradman, but he had to wait until the cheering stopped. His second ball, a full toss, Bradman nimbly straight drove to the boundary.

The bowler at the other end was Statham, who recalls: "We all wanted to see more. I worked out that the best way was to bowl at three-quarter pace, straight and keep the ball well pitched up. This would minimize the chance of his getting an edge and giving a catch." Bradman middled Statham's first ball, even though it kept a bit low.

Of his second ball, the bowler says that Bradman "played a little outside it, snicked it on to his pads and was bowled through his legs." The ball only trickled into the stumps. Statham continues: "I was horrified. I wheeled round to the umpire: 'Come on! Shout no-ball.' It was too late. Sir Don was already on his way back. The day had been ruined."

The bowler called it the worst delivery of his life. But Bradman said: "It might have happened once in a thousand times." And in any case the match was an all-round success.

With a bit of connivance, an exciting finish ensued, though it looked unlikely in Statham's next over when Harvey was caught by Sheppard off a skier to mid wicket: 122 for 6. The *Manchester Evening News,* loyally but tongue-in-cheek, pointed out that 'in successive overs, Statham had dismissed Australia's greatest pre-war and post-war batsmen'.

Statham bowled only three overs, taking 2 for 13, but poor Bedser not only was denied a bowl at his former adversary, Bradman, but also finished with 1 for 79 off 10.4 overs.

That it was an exhibition type of game was emphasized by Cowdrey being posted to the long on boundary, and by Mackay, of all batsmen, hitting 49 in 25 minutes!

Benaud scored 68 but he was determined that MCC, who had entered into the spirit of the occasion so well, should win. Although the younger fielders had been dropping easy catches in order to rig a close finish, Benaud got himself out with half an hour to go, and Bedser made a fine one-handed catch at mid off to dismiss Grout.

MCC finally won by three runs, but of course the real winner was, as planned, charity.

Fading from the Test Scene

EVEN though the weather and Lancashire's performances were nearly as bad in 1963 as in 1962, Statham's bowling improved to the extent that his average came down from 23 to 15, as he took over 100 Championship wickets.

Joe Blackledge retired, and Grieves returned to Lancashire as their new captain. He and Statham were fortunate in that Peter Lever, in his first full season, showed much promise, because Colin Hilton hardly appeared and Higgs again failed to progress.

The county's opening fixture was noteworthy — the first-ever Gillette Cup match, a preliminary game to reduce the total of contestants from 17 to 16. Lancashire and Leicestershire had to compete because they had been the bottom two in the previous Championship! At Old Trafford on 1 May, the match was delayed by rain until 3pm. In cold weather, Lancashire were put in to bat but they made 304 for 9 in the 65 overs, with Marner scoring 121, including the biggest six that Statham ever saw at the ground — it landed towards the ten-pin bowling alley.

The next day Leicester began their quest on a drier pitch. Of course, Statham was not a pleasant proposition when runs were needed quickly. He opened with a six-over spell and took three wickets. Without conceding a run in the actual process, he bowled Bird off stump and had Wharton and Jayasinghe caught at the wicket, all playing forward. Hallam led Leicester to 162 for 4, at which point Statham returned. The bowler still had nine overs left, the limit at that time being 15 overs per bowler. However, the task of reaching more than 300 in time was beyond the visitors, and Higgs and Marner helped Statham (who bowled two tail-enders) to take Lancashire to victory.

Statham finished with 12-2-28-5 and this is still the best analysis of any Lancashire bowler in the Gillette Cup, in spite of the fact that the player did not win the 'Man of the Match' award for it! Frank Woolley selected Marner, for his century and 3 for 49.

Later in May, Statham took ten wickets in a match for the only time in the season — against Northants at Rushden. On the first day, both sides were dismissed on a pitch of green patches and varying softness. The ball came through at differing heights, especially at the end to which Larter and then Statham bowled. Larter took 6 for 52 of Lancashire's 100 all out. Northants reached 30 before Statham bowled Reynolds with a ball which kept low. Norman, often beaten, survived to score 37 before Statham dismissed him. In a later spell, the England bowler took three wickets at a cost of two runs, to finish with 20-10-31-5 of Northants' 135.

A fine century by Grieves enabled Lancashire to set the home side 217 to win. On the last morning, Northants soon found the task difficult. Reynolds fell to Statham, who also saw Norman and Ramsamooj snick him to the slips and escape. But then he bowled Ramsamooj, had Jim Watts leg-before to a shooter, and bowled Prideaux, which gave him 4 for 22 so far, and at lunch Northants were 63 for 6.

It was unfortunate that the pitch was so inconsistent that many players and officials thought it was below first-class standard. Sometimes the ball rose shoulder high.

After lunch, Lightfoot resisted, though Higgs bowled two of his partners. Lightfoot drove Statham for a three and a four, as rain clouds gathered. Then he played forward to a ball which reared up and hit him in the face. He fell on his stumps and was carried off with a cut and shock.

Then rain stopped play at 79 and during the ten-minute delay, the umpires announced that Lightfoot, because he had completed his shot before hitting his stumps was not out. However, this was academic because the batsman was not well enough to continue. At 83 for 8, there was a 20-minute stoppage, but then there was a bit of sun and Statham finished the match by sending Larter's off stump hurtling. His 5 for 37 gave him 10 for 68 in the match from 41 overs. Higgs' support, especially in the second innings, was also praiseworthy.

On 6 June, Statham played on his home ground in the First Test against the West Indies. It was not a happy Test for him.

On a pitch which *The Times* described as a 'treasure-house of runs', with little pace and only the slightest early moisture, Statham 'rarely worried the batsmen', said *Wisden*. He did beat the bat occasionally, but to no avail. Trueman was more hostile, but neither bowler found the correct length immediately.

In a cold wind, Statham was soon faced with a skied catch sent by Carew, who mis-hooked Trueman to mid on when he was ten. After a long wait, Statham put it down. *The Times* said that to see him miss a catch was 'like spotting a great crested grebe in the middle of Manchester', and *Wisden* thought it might have upset his bowling. But Carew quickly fell to Trueman anyway, and only in the afternoon, in front of 16,000 spectators, did the West Indies capitalize on the winning of the toss.

Kanhai led the way when, having reached 50, he added another 40 in 50 minutes. After tea, the fast bowlers took the new ball, but bad light and then rain stopped play at 244 for 3. Hunte, the anchorman, was 104 not out; Statham's figures for the day were 17-4-56-0.

On the second day, the weather gradually improved and on what *The Guardian* called a 'mercilessly' good pitch, even Statham and Trueman bowled defensively. The West Indies advanced to 336 at lunch without further loss. In the last over before the interval, Sobers hooked Statham for six, but on the resumption, the Lancashire bowler sent down eight overs for 21 runs, beating Hunte four times off the pitch, and Solomon twice before he had scored. *The Times* called it a magnificent spell, and it was with the old ball — his partner was Allen (who also bowled well) rather than Trueman.

Hunte was finally out for 182 at 398 for 5, which brought Worrell to the crease. At 3.45pm the third new ball was due, but the visiting captain was in great form, encouraged by being dropped at slip off Statham (when 35) and off Trueman. He scored 74 not out in 95 minutes, which included, in one Statham over after tea, three late cuts which sent the ball to the boundary almost too quickly to be seen.

At 5.30pm, Worrell declared at 501 for 6, and he received a great ovation, partly due no doubt to his links and associations with Lancashire people. And in the background was Statham, who had so often dismissed Worrell in Tests, but who now left the field with figures on the day of 20-2-65-0 and in the innings of 37-6-121-0. This was one of the least successful efforts of his career.

Yet, in the face of much fine batting on such a plumb pitch, the four main England bowlers 'performed creditably', said *Wisden.*

The pitch later took spin at England's expense, so that the West Indies went on to win by ten wickets.

For the Lord's Test ten days later, Statham was replaced by Shackleton. During very few of 13 English summers and eight tours abroad had a fit Statham been dropped by England. Reviewing the bowler's long Test career, John Arlott decided that "but for Trueman, we should call him unique." But clearly the Lancashire bowler was now, in the very nature of things, nearing the end of his England days.

To the comments on Statham's disappointing form in Australia, Arlott adds that the bowler could in 1963 "no longer sustain his former penetration through a five-day Test on a slow pitch; and, at heart, he did not want to."

But England's tactics also contributed to the discarding of Statham, who after all was now being replaced by a bowler of a different type. The plan was to test the West Indian batsmen not simply with fast bowling, but also with fast-medium seam bowling backed by English conditions. Shackleton's was the epitome of the latter type, and of course the West Indians were much less used to it.

I discount the fact that Lord's, which Cowdrey called a 'seamer's paradise' at this period, suited Shackleton — because it also suited Statham. The Lancashire bowler's Test record at Lord's was better than at any other venue, and he calls it his favourite of all grounds.

But Shackleton's case must have been strengthened by his performance at Lord's during, ironically, the Old Trafford Test. For Hampshire against Middlesex, he bowled unchanged throughout and had these analyses: 27-14-34-5 and 33-20-42-5.

Since Statham was regarded by some as unlucky to lose his place — for example, by Brian Close and by the editor of *Wisden* — it is important to record that in the Lord's Test, Shackleton now bowled very well. He kept his place for the rest of the series. Trueman, for his part, bowled brilliantly at both Lord's and Edgbaston, taking 23 wickets in two successive Tests!

For the final Test at The Oval, Statham was recalled, to join Trueman and Shackleton. But none of them (although Trueman was injured for the second innings) could prevent the West Indies, already 2-1 up in the rubber, from winning the match. Statham's figures were 3 for 68 (Worrell, bowled Statham 9) and 0 for 54.

In between his two Test appearances, Statham took plenty of wickets for his county. Perhaps his performance at The Oval against

Surrey, a week before the final Test, did most to earn him his England place back. The rain-interrupted first day 'belonged almost entirely to Statham', said *The Guardian.* He began, encouraged by the movement off the pitch he was obtaining, by bowling three England batsmen off stump, each for single figures: Stewart, Edrich and Barrington, who were out in Statham's first, fourth and seventh overs respectively.

After lunch, though not moving the ball so much, he ended a recovery stand by taking his 100th wicket of the season, Willett. In the same over, he also dismissed Parsons; and when he had Tindall leg-before a few runs later, he had taken all the first six Surrey wickets for 48 out of a total of 136 for 6. But then Tony Lock hit 60 in 45 minutes, including 4 fours in one over from Statham! So the fast bowler's analysis finally read 27-4-96-7. But the match was ruined by rain, and the only decision was that Lancashire gained first-innings points.

With figures of 6 for 28 in the following game at Buxton, also rain-spoilt, Statham had form on his side for the Test at The Oval. But as we have seen, the West Indies were too good, which was perhaps the story of the summer for both Statham and England.

Consolation at Leicester

STATHAM was not chosen for any of the 1964 Tests against Australia, although there was no obvious replacement for him. Flavell, Coldwell, John Price and Fred Rumsey were all tried — as Larter and Jeff Jones had also been, in India a few months previously. As for Trueman, he was England's most successful bowler against Australia, even though he had one poor Test, after which he was temporarily dropped.

Nor did Statham appear in his county's match against the Australians, so he never played against the touring side. In that respect, this season was unique in his career.

Thus his play was basically limited to Championship games, and he showed his continued fitness by missing only two of them. He bowled more overs for Lancashire in this summer than in any other, the result being 109 wickets at 20 runs each. But as to his team, there was a jinx over them, as there had been in 1962. The Centenary of the club's formation in 1864 counted for nothing.

Though the weather, at least later in the season, was kinder, Lancashire finished low down the table again, and were torn by internal strife. The committee, the new team manager (Washbrook), the captain (Grieves) and the players failed to work in unison. But Statham was one of several players who nevertheless managed to succeed individually.

On 9 June at Bristol, Lancashire nearly achieved their first win of the season in a very close match. The Saturday had been rained off and on the Monday, Gloucestershire reached 52 for 2 in reply to Lancashire's 194 for 9 declared. The deficit for follow-on purposes being 100 in such a reduced match, the home team's prime target was 95, but Statham caused them anxiety on the last morning.

Having bowled the night-watchman, he also bowled the next three men for ducks: a spell of four wickets for three runs in seven overs. Gloucester were then 69 for 6 and they found 95 quite enough to get. But each side was able to make a declaration and the outcome was an exciting, evenly-balanced draw. In Gloucester's second innings, Statham bowled three more men, including Bissex first ball for the second time in one day!

A week or so later, Statham bowled well at Peterborough late on the first day — his birthday. In the first over of Northamptonshire's reply, he had Reynolds caught. He proceeded to send back Prideaux, leg-before without offering a stroke, Lightfoot and Jim Watts. This gave him 4 for 9 out of the home team's 13 for 5, and he finished with 6 for 27 out of 55 all out. However, rain prevented a result.

In July, Lancashire gained their first two Championship wins of the season, and then met Middlesex at Old Trafford. Rain interrupted the match and when Middlesex declared at 217 for 8, Lancashire were faced with an unpredictable pitch, and a strong wind which blew straight down the wicket from the Stretford end. These conditions helped to fool the home batsmen, and Lancashire had collapsed to a mere 26 for 7 when Statham went out to bat. *The Guardian* described his now successful policy thus: 'everything overpitched he hit hard; he never assumed how a short ball would behave'.

Of course, his innings was lucky too — he missed or edged the ball, and his boundary-hit to bring up his side's 50 was not far from being a catch to mid on. But he hit 8 fours (six of them good ones!) including three in an over from Clark. His 52 in 70 minutes took Lancashire to 103 all out, and the next highest scorer made 13. The outcome of the match was that Lancashire later made a fine attempt to reach the target they had been set, and they lost by only 12 runs.

A fortnight later, Lancashire played at the Courtaulds ground at Coventry which, as Statham well knew, usually favoured pace bowling. On the first evening, Warwickshire replied to Lancashire's 191 with 21 for 3; Statham had Horner caught in the gully and Ibadulla leg-before, while Higgs dismissed Bob Barber.

The next morning, after the night-watchman had been run out, Statham had Jameson leg-before and then at 48 he had Jim Stewart superbly caught by Grieves, one-handed at second slip. When he had Hitchcock and Amiss also caught, he had taken 6 for 23 out of the home side's 59 for 8. But then Alan Smith and Mence brought about a recovery: 89 for 8 at lunch, 108 for 8 when the opening bowlers were finally replaced, and 155 all out when Statham had Mence caught, after the number-ten had reached his maiden first-class 50. The bowler's analysis was 29.3-8-50-7. However, Warwickshire's fine second-innings batting gave them victory, which they soon repeated in a controversial Gillette Cup semi-final.

In early August, at Grace Road, Leicester, Statham produced one of the best performances of his career. Leicestershire chose to bat, although the green pitch soon proved lively. Statham had Brian Booth, who had just left Lancashire, leg-before with his fifth delivery — *The Guardian* reported that the ball moved one way in the air and another off the pitch. With the score at 26, after a brief stoppage due to a shower, Graham Cross played too late at a Statham break-back which uprooted his off stump.

The same bowler hit the off stump again at 42, when Inman drove and missed. Higgs at this stage was bowling without luck, and not until 89, after another break for rain and one for lunch, did the fourth wicket fall when Statham had van Geloven caught at slip after a fumble.

When Greensword went for a duck, the fast bowler had taken all the first five wickets in an unchanged, though interrupted, spell of 20 overs in two and a half hours. But Jayasinghe had been attacking the bowling, and he went on to 64, before Ramadhin (a new Lancashire recruit) bowled him and then dismissed Kirby.

Leicester came back with a late stand, which ended when Statham removed Julian's off stump at 184 for 8. This brought Spencer to the crease in his Benefit match and Statham gave him a leg side full toss as a special privilege, before bowling him! When the home side declared at 197 for 9, Statham's analysis was 29.2-10-71-7, and *The Guardian* thought that he had still bowled well within himself — clearly profitable tactics in the damp conditions.

But Lancashire were now all out with a first innings deficit of 20, and late on the Monday Leicester went in again. The pitch was still helping the pace bowlers and furthermore showing signs of wear. Statham soon bowled van Geloven and Cross, while Higgs had Booth lbw. Then Statham sent back four men in quick succession, helped by fine catches by Marner and Grieves in the slips and Higgs in the gully. Leicester were now 42 for 7 and reached 54 for 7 (Statham 6 for 27) at the close of the second day.

There was no escape for the home team on the last morning. Statham quickly dismissed Julian and sent Spencer's leg stump flying, and Higgs completed the rout at 69. Statham's figures in the innings were 17-2-37-8 (the second best of his career), and in the match, 15 for 108 (also his second best). Lancashire needed 90 to win, and they succeeded, but it was only their fourth Championship victory (and their last) of the summer.

Reviewing the completed season, I find the 1964 Lancashire bowling averages raise a point. Each year two lists are published, one for Championship matches, and the other for all Lancashire's first-class matches. Statham had been top of the latter list for every year from 1951 to 1963 inclusive, even though he had, in two of those years, not topped the Championship list.

In 1964, Greenhough topped the Championship averages in his Benefit year, with 27 wickets at 18.85. He would also have headed Statham in Lancashire's all-match averages, except that the Lancashire Year Books stipulate a minimum of 40 wickets for that list.

Thus, given that qualification, Statham now topped that list for the 14th consecutive year. No other Lancashire player had, or has, exceeded Richard Tyldesley's not-quite-consecutive eight times.

Now for a wider issue. I have already said that in 1964 the personnel at Old Trafford were not functioning as a unit, and I could up to a point have said the same about the preceding few years. But now, with continued poor results on the field and a decline in discipline, self-discipline and team spirit among both players and administrators, matters came to a head.

This showdown was mainly the work of an ordinary member — Cedric Rhoades. His efforts, made within the rules of the club, led to the resignation of the committee in late 1964. The new committee of 12 which was elected included six of the former committee, but the man with the most votes was Rhoades himself. (He was to become chairman in 1969). Along with the club's constitution and finances, one of the most important items on the new committee's agenda was the team captaincy.

Grieves had already been relieved of the leadership as the season ended, and towards the end of 1964 — and strictly during the interregnum between the old and the new committees — the following notice appeared in *The Times:*

> *'A first-class county cricket club invites applications from persons with first-class cricket experience for the position of captain of the county XI. The position will carry a salary in accordance with experience and an allowance to cover expenses.'*

When John Kay revealed that the box number was Lancashire's, many people associated with the club took exception to the advertisement.

Ken Grieves called it "an insult to Brian Statham."

A Man Possessed

AND Grieves knew what he was talking about. Whose applications were received in the wake of the advertisement, was not disclosed. Be that as it may, the new committee, when they had settled in early in 1965, offered the captaincy to the man on their doorstep whose experience in cricket was second to none — Brian Statham.

As the bowler points out, he had not sought the honour. But his attitude was that "there is still a lot I can do for Lancashire, and when the call came for me to skipper the side in the hour of their greatest need, I needed no second bidding."

Good luck messages poured in from cricketers and cricket lovers all over the world — and he said he intended to answer them all!

He then set out his own wish: "My final contribution to cricket will, I hope, be to lead Lancashire back to a respectable place in the Championship table." But his promise could only be: "Lancashire will play cricket in the right spirit."

He did not have any illusions — he knew the limitations of his players, especially in batting and close fielding. He knew that he would no longer be able to rest at third man after bowling, but would have to direct operations from mid off. And he wrote: "Getting wickets in Tests was never easy, but getting Lancashire back to the top will be my toughest job in cricket."

And let me interject a comment on captaincy, written by Statham a few years earlier and showing his sympathy for the men he had played under: "Yet how, with life going round him ten times faster than it goes round anyone else, does the skipper stay human and likeable through it all? It's a great tribute to the durability of human nature."

I have called Statham 'a man possessed' in the 1965 season because he now, at a late stage in his career and after several relatively disappointing seasons, reached almost new heights.

His achievements were in bowling rather than in captaincy, but clearly the latter appointment galvanized him. It also stimulated the new-look team, even though the playing results only improved slightly. *Wisden* said that 'under Statham's inspiring leadership a new spirit of keen endeavour was always apparent'. *The Guardian* correspondent asked during August: 'Has any other Lancashire captain set such an inspiring example?'

John Kay pointed out that many people had originally "insisted that Statham could not combine his duties as the club's leading wicket-taker with those of the captaincy." But in the event the bowler was now, for the only season in his career, the first man in the country to take a hundred wickets; and his number of victims for Lancashire — 130, and at only 12.08 each — was greater than in any other year.

Statham was helped by the not very summery conditions, which often favoured seam bowling, by underprepared pitches and by Higgs, who returned to his peak of 1960. The pair certainly combined to their mutual advantage in 1965. The senior partner wrote at the time: "No captain ever had a greater trier than Higgs in his side"; while *The Times* wrote that Higgs 'has learnt from Statham what it means to try'. Their combined total of 244 wickets for the county would have been even more, given commensurate slip-catching. But few Lancashire opening pairs have ever enjoyed such a successful season as Statham and Higgs did in 1965 (or, for that matter, in 1960). One would perhaps, given that the fast-slow combination of Mold and Briggs was unique, pick out Brearley and Kermode (in 1905) and Phillipson and Pollard (in 1939) to stand comparison.

As for the details of the season, Statham, having previously captained a first-class team only occasionally, led Lancashire at Taunton for their first match of the new campaign. They lost, but the next match — against the New Zealanders at Old Trafford starting on 8 May — was more encouraging.

As *Wisden* reports, nothing went right for the tourists. There was so much rain about that not only was there a blank Saturday, but the original pitch became saturated. Groundsman Bert Flack had to attempt to prepare an adjacent one instead. But he did not really have enough time — so the new pitch had too little mowing and too little rolling.

John Reid, having won the toss, was influenced by the green pitch, the dew and the haze and put Lancashire in to bat. However, as play went on, especially on the damp Monday and Tuesday mornings, the top surface of the hurriedly-prepared pitch cut up more and more. So the county had the best of the pitch, such as it was, and they scored 225 on the Monday, to which the New Zealanders replied with 50 for 1 by the close.

On the Tuesday morning they collapsed to 76 for 6, at which point Dick and Motz started attacking because they thought they had avoided the follow-on. At 114 for 8, Reid, from the balcony, signalled a declaration. But Statham called out to Reid, 'sportingly' said *Wisden,* that in a two-day match the follow-on deficit was reduced to 100. In other words, the visitors had needed not 76 but 126. Batting on, they fell short by 11 runs, hampered by the absence of Vivian because of an ankle injury.

Thus, 18 minutes before lunch on this last day, the tourists started their follow-on — and sank deeper into the mire. After a leg bye, Statham's sixth ball, breaking back, had Congdon lbw. Then Higgs accounted for Dowling, and Statham had Morgan caught off a lifter which went from bat to pad to short leg. The lunchtime score was one run for three wickets.

After the interval, Reid and Sutcliffe had added only seven runs more when their team met even more trouble. Statham removed the captain's off stump, and his next ball pitched on Dick's leg stump before hitting the off. The bowler later apologetically called this delivery an unplayable fluke. Half the side were out for eight and Statham had dismissed four of them at a cost of two runs. Then, without addition, Sutcliffe was caught behind off Higgs. The score-card then read:

New Zealanders		
G.Dowling	lbw b Higgs	0
B.Congdon	lbw b Statham	0
R.Morgan	c Worsley b Statham	0
J.Reid	b Statham	3
B.Sutcliffe	c Goodwin b Higgs	4
A.Dick	b Statham	0
B.Taylor	not out	0
V.Pollard	not out	0
Extras	(l-b)	1
Total	**(6 wickets)**	**8**

After this, the opening bowlers, as if either in sympathy for the visitors' ill luck, or in excitement at the threat to first-class cricket's lowest-ever total of 12 all out, lost some of their accuracy. When Statham removed Taylor's middle stump the total was 24 for 7, but the New Zealanders, even though they were a batsman short, recovered even more, thanks to Pollard, Motz and Cameron.

Statham had rested Higgs and himself from the attack soon after the fall of the seventh wicket but, Greenhough having dismissed Motz, the pair returned late in the day. Higgs bowled Pollard at 104, which gave Lancashire victory by an innings and six runs, with 20 minutes of normal time to spare. Statham's analysis was 10-5-15-5.

Each captain was generous to the other after the match. Statham wrote that "even the best bad-wicket players would have been in trouble and the New Zealanders had the worst of the pitch." And he emphasized that pitches in New Zealand are always covered.

John Reid praised the county for their first win over a touring side for many years — in fact, since victory over the 1937 New Zealanders.

Gloucestershire visited Old Trafford later in May, and *Wisden* said: 'Despite a pitch of easy pace, Statham bowled magnificently on the opening day'. In bright but chilly weather, play was uneventful until the second new ball appeared just after tea. At 161 for 3, Statham made a ball lift and move away from Bissex, who was well caught at first slip by Beddow. Statham then bowled Mortimore middle stump for a duck, and uprooted the same peg while it was in the brief custody of Windows. In between, he had made a ball leave Milton, who was taken in the gully for 77.

This was a spell of four wickets for three runs with his first 25 deliveries with the new ball, and Gloucester were now 175 for 7. But the visitors staged a fine late rally, and it was not until the next morning that Statham took the last three wickets — and even then, not in quick succession. His final analysis was one of his best: 33.1-10-69-8, but Gloucester's 286 turned out to be enough to win them the match.

At Lord's a fortnight later (just after his first win as captain), Statham reduced Middlesex to 23 for 3 when they replied on the first evening to Lancashire's 174. His 3 for 7 spell included the trapping of Russell and Brearley leg-before, and the bowling of the night-watchman. Referring to this evening's play, *The Times* later in the season reported the comment that in the first 12 overs from Statham and Higgs, all but two balls had to be played. The next day, on a good pitch, Statham took his innings figures to 6 for 38 in 25 overs. But on the last afternoon it was the enterprising Middlesex batsmen who won the match with 15 minutes to spare (though for some reason the captain underbowled himself at this stage).

Later in June, at Buxton, the first day belonged to the pace bowlers of both sides. On a cloudy day which included a short break for rain, first Brian Jackson and Rhodes, and then Statham and Higgs, were responsible for a major batting collapse. The pitch was at a drying stage for both sets of bowlers and it never eased all day.

The need to realign the wickets, a foot out because there was no theodolite, perhaps helped to confuse the Lancashire batsmen! They were all out for 88, although they lasted 57 overs so, with the realignment and the rain, the innings took until around teatime.

Statham began Lancashire's retaliation by removing Eyre's off stump with the score at 5, but though he continued unchanged with Higgs, Derbyshire had managed to reach 57 for 4 by 6.20pm. Then at that score the home team lost four wickets, and by 6.50pm were 61 all out! The captain's last 6.1 overs produced five wickets for four runs and his final analysis was 18.5-9-16-6. Higgs had supported him superbly while the pair, backed by good catching, had bowled throughout the innings of two and a quarter hours. The crowd applauded them both generously.

The visitors had their two points, but the weather allowed a second innings only to Lancashire and so prevented a likely close finish.

A week's rest from representative cricket seemed to benefit Lancashire, judging by their performance at Old Trafford against Nottinghamshire on 30 June. They scored 302 for 4, declaring overnight, and in the visitors' reply of 241, Statham bowled five men at a cost of 52 runs.

After Lancashire had followed with 156, Nottinghamshire required 218 to win in 205 minutes, starting at 1.10pm on the last day, admittedly with the handicaps of a rain-affected pitch and light which was to worsen.

On the stroke of lunchtime, Statham had Bolus lbw, and in the early afternoon removed Millman's off stump and had Moore caught. Having bowled flat out for an hour and a half, interrupted by lunch, Statham struck again towards 3.30pm. In his 15th over he dismissed both Whittingham and Maurice Hill, so he had taken all the five wickets Nottinghamshire had lost in reaching 67. Lancashire, well on top, had about 1¾ hours, that is until 5.15pm (tea being waived), to capture the other five for their second Championship win under the new captain.

The spinners took two wickets each, and Statham took another in between thanks to a fine catch by 'keeper Goodwin: 109 all out with 15 minutes to spare. The Nottinghamshire players on the balcony joined in the applause for Statham as he led the way in. His analysis was 18-4-36-6, which gave him 11 for 88 in the match.

At Hove on 26 July, Statham became the first bowler to take a hundred wickets in the season as he, Higgs and Lever caused a Sussex second-innings collapse, although Lancashire could not quite turn it into victory. On an unreliable pitch, the captain finished with 5 for 38, the milestone being reached when he bowled Graves. A cluster of pace bowlers had taken round about 80 wickets by July 24th (when Statham had captured 95), but not until the first week of August did any of them reach 100. *Wisden* gives Statham's opinion: 'While he agreed that he had bowled well, he said the main reason for his success had been the atrocious pitches he had met here and there'.

On 14 August, the Championship leaders of the moment, Northamptonshire, came to Old Trafford. That they won by ten wickets was no fault of Statham's. On a green pitch and in a hazy atmosphere, he and Higgs were lethal with the new ball. *The Guardian* thought the sight of all Statham's skills and tactics would have delighted Lindwall himself.

In the captain's third over, Reynolds played a lifting ball to gully, where Steele was also soon caught. In between, Statham bowled Prideaux with an inswinger. This spell was 3 for 14 in seven overs, and when Peter Watts, already dropped at slip off Statham, was bowled by Higgs, Northampton were 30 for 4.

During the opening bowlers' second spell each side of lunch, Higgs bowled Milburn, and Statham with a perfect-length ball bettered Jim Watts' good-looking forward stroke: 85 for 6. But now the bowlers were tiring and the visitors were let off the hook. *The*

Guardian reporter denounced the 'pointlessness of preparing a fast bowlers' pitch and then picking only two fast bowlers'. He thought that if Lever had been also selected, Northants might not have even reached 100. As it was, Lightfoot and Crump added 124 in a seventh-wicket stand, ended by Statham with the new ball, by means of a fine caught and bowled. Finally, the visitors were all out for 231 in the evening, Statham dismissing two tail-enders for an analysis of 26.2-10-47-7.

The next day, Lancashire, however, collapsed to off-spin, failed by one run to avoid the follow-on, and lost the match badly. The county finished the season in 13th place, only one place higher than in 1964 — yet improvement in their team spirit and effort under Statham was widely recognized.

As for the Test Match scene, a three-match New Zealand series was followed by a similar one against South Africa. England, influenced partly by the coming tour of Australia, had experimented with different fast bowling combinations all summer. Trueman had played in two Tests, his last two as it transpired; Rumsey and Larter had played in several; and Snow and David Brown had won their first caps.

Of all this, Statham wrote at the start of the second Test against South Africa: "Short of giving Ken Higgs a run and asking me to come back, there are few other bowling permutations yet to be tried." He believed Higgs was worthy of selection, but regarding himself he thought: "There is really no point in turning the clock back." This confirms the opinion he had given in the spring to *The Times,* that he hoped 'for England's sake' that his recall would not be necessary. And in the spring too he had announced that he would not be available for the tour of Australia in any event.

Moreover, in mid-season Statham had written: "Fast bowling is no job for old men in Test cricket these days. I know what it means bowling flat out for Lancashire, without aspiring to greater heights in my cricketing old age."

But after England had lost the second South Africa Test, the need to square the series eclipsed any team-building considerations. Furthermore, an injury to Larter made him unavailable for the third and final Test. The selectors might have chosen Snow, Rumsey, Flavell, Coldwell or Jeff Jones. But in fact they now chose a man who had been out of Tests for two years but whose exceptional current form they recognized: Statham. They also chose David Brown and Cartwright among their 12 for The Oval.

The Guardian's opinion on Statham was: 'As Lancashire's captain, he has bowled with a zest and conviction which a year ago he seemed to have lost', and that he was still often genuinely fast and might well have ousted Larter even if the latter had been fit.

The Times, dubbing him 'that reluctant hero', said: 'Everyone will be delighted to see Statham back under the colours, no one more than Mike Smith. For 12 years, Statham was his captain's staunchest friend.'

The bowler himself said that he had never expected another chance. He said he was very nervous on the morning of the match, although *The Times* reported that on his arrival the day before, he strolled to the nets 'looking as relaxed as ever, though a little thinner and perhaps a little greyer'.

Statham must have been pleased at the choice of Cartwright's replacement, when the latter had to withdraw from the 12 owing to a thumb injury. The replacement was the uncapped Ken Higgs, whom Statham had recommended to the selectors in a recent article in the *Manchester Evening News*. With a view to the coming tour of Australia in particular, his captain had written of Higgs: 'No spell is too long for him. No batsman ever worries him.' And one reader had been so impressed that he had persuaded the newspaper to forward a copy of the article direct to the selectors!

The first day of the Test, 26 August, was cloudy with a cool breeze. It was announced that Higgs was to gain his first cap, Allen being 12th man. The pitch was quite well-grassed, but because it did not look very green and because the atmosphere was not humid, Mike Smith's decision to field seemed bold. *Wisden* called the pitch slow and never really difficult, though it did produce some movement.

Statham bowled the first over to Barlow, and the fifth ball, pitched further up, brought a rejected appeal for lbw. After four overs each from Statham and Brown, Higgs replaced Statham, who thus changed ends. Now the Lancashire pair broke through. Higgs, in only his third over in Tests, dismissed Lindsay, and at 12.30pm Statham, with a ball which moved in slightly, had Barlow lbw. The score was 23 for 2, Statham's wicket having cost him, in eight overs, only eight runs.

Graeme Pollock, the hero of South Africa's win in the previous Test, now came in and cover drove Statham for a four which even the bowler applauded. Bacher also hit Statham for two fours, but when the bowler's opening spell ended after 80 minutes' play, *The Times* thought he had hardly wasted a ball. Pollock soon fell to Titmus, but Bland retaliated with a six, before lunch came at 72 for 3.

After the interval, with the crowd building up to 20,000, Bland at once hit Titmus high and straight again. Statham at long on reached the ball and caught it high and right-handed. But the fielder's fine effort counted for nought, or rather six, because he had crossed the boundary rope in the act.

At 86, Higgs dismissed Bacher and at 2.40pm Statham returned. The latter now got the better of Bland by keeping him both quiet and away from Titmus, and at about 3.00pm, Statham cornered Bland on the back foot to a ball pitching near the blockhole. The batsman was out leg-before, Statham having 'yorked his pads', in *The Guardian's* phrase. Then at 128 for 5 at about 3.40pm, bad light stopped play. Tea was taken, but only another half-hour's cricket was possible, and play ended at 152 for 5 with drizzle around.

Statham's figures for the day were 17-9-32-2 and *The Times* said that he, 'as everyone knew he would, bowled beautifully. He was scarcely slower than of old and no less rhythmic.' The same reporter found Higgs' 15-3-24-2 most heartening.

On the second morning, the pitch was more responsive as a result of the rain. Higgs dismissed van der Merwe and, with the new ball, Dumbrill. Statham then had Botten well taken at first slip by Cowdrey, and bowled Peter Pollock. He closed the innings by trapping top-scorer Lance leg-before, to become only the second bowler to reach a total of 250 Test wickets. His morning spell was 7.2-2-8-3 and his innings analysis 24.2-11-40-5. The England players waited for the two Lancashire men (nine wickets between them) to lead the team off the field.

England replied to South Africa's 208 with a lacklustre 202 and the visitors began their second innings during the Saturday morning. Statham bowled Barlow off stump immediately after lunch, but Bacher led South Africa to a sound 163 for 3 by close of play.

Bacher was out to the first ball he received on the Monday morning, when, in Statham's opening over, the batsman turned the ball to Smith at short leg. However, the rest of the day belonged to Bland, who went on to 127; his front-foot play was compared by *The Times* to that of Dexter and Hammond. Bland treated the new ball with disdain. Statham was hit, mainly by Bland, for 24 runs in his first four overs with it. South Africa batted until after tea, making 392, in which Statham's analysis was 29-1-105-2, and Higgs' a creditable 41.1-9-96-4. England were left with a target of 399 in seven hours.

Fortunately for the crowd, the England batsmen changed gear and made an exciting attempt, reaching 290 for 4 by tea on the last day. By 4.50pm, with 70 minutes and six wickets left, 91 runs were wanted to square the series. But I need only add one more word: rain.

Despite his disappointing figures in South Africa's second innings, Statham, if he had been available, might well have been selected for the 1965-6 tour of Australia. His first-innings performance at The Oval had been most impressive, and typical of the success he had been meeting with all the summer.

He finished the season with 137 first-class wickets, which was only two short of his best-ever total (in 1959, when he had bowled 200 overs more). And his striking-rate in 1965 was his best-ever (a wicket about every 5½ overs). He was third in the national averages with 12.52; and he had taken five wickets in an innings 14 times, which was more than in any other season.

However, one appreciates that Statham owed it to himself to scotch any possibility of yet another tour to Australia. So, in a cricket sense, he rested for once on his laurels.

Bowled Statham, CBE

ON New Year's Day 1966, Statham became the first bowler to be awarded the CBE. Other cricketers had received knighthoods and other cricketers had received CBE's, but none of them were mere bowlers. Statham had recently written, influenced by a featherbed Test pitch made for batsmen: "I know from past experience that nobody loves a bowler." Perhaps this award, like a lively pitch, helped him to overcome such a feeling!

His name appeared in the Prime Minister's List, between those of a Medical Officer of Health and a Chief Inspector of Schools. The award was 'for services to cricket'. Statham was reported as being overwhelmed, and saying: "It's a great honour to cricket in general and myself in particular. I feel I ought to share it with my colleagues in the Lancashire and England teams these past 15 years."

As captain of Lancashire in 1966, he 'again led the side most ably', reported the Committee. During a wet summer, the playing results improved only slightly, the main problem being the batting. In *Wisden*, John Kay wrote that "Lancashire's inability to score steadily constantly nullified the splendid efforts of their seam attack."

Statham enjoyed a notable match in the county's first win, against Nottinghamshire at Old Trafford in May. Though the pitch started easy-paced, the visitors were all out for 113 (Statham 3 for 28); Lancashire, with the new 65-over limit in force, replied with 160 for 5. Nottingham's second innings began shortly before lunch on the second day, and Norman Hill was soon run out.

Just after the interval, Swetman played back to Statham, missed and was lbw, giving the bowler his 2,000th first-class wicket. Statham thus followed, among wholly post-1945 players, Lock, Shackleton, Trueman and Bailey to the milestone. And his average was such that it remains the best of any post-1945 bowler who has taken even 1,000 wickets; and the best of any post-1918 bowler who has taken 2,000 wickets.

Nottinghamshire slumped to 65 for 5 but Moore batted well until

Higgs had him caught (117 for 6) just before tea. After tea, Statham bowled three tail-enders in seven balls, the visitors were all out for 125 (Statham 20-8-31-5), and Lancashire won easily.

The next home county match, against Glamorgan on 11 June, was at Aigburth, Liverpool, a ground usually favouring bowlers. Indeed, when umpire Bill Copson, the former Derbyshire fast bowler then aged 57, saw the green pitch, he said: "I might get four or five wickets on that myself — even now." The two captains, also fast bowlers, Statham and Ossie Wheatley, were equally enthusiastic. Glamorgan won the toss and, in cloudy, humid weather, put Lancashire in. The home team reached 139 for 7 in their 65 overs, having resisted appealing against the light.

Glamorgan, going in at about 3.30pm, did appeal — after only two balls from Statham. The appeal was rejected and next ball Alan Jones was bowled off stump. Then Higgs accounted for Roger Davis, and Statham had Peter Walker and Tony Lewis each leg-before, though the latter may have been unlucky in the decision. The captain had taken 3 for 11 of Glamorgan's 25 for 4. After tea, he, Higgs and Lever took another wicket each and the visitors finished the day at 88 for 7. On the Monday morning, Glamorgan were all out for 99, Statham bowling Shepherd and, with his next ball, Jeff Jones. He finished with 22.1-9-41-6, by virtue of swing and seam. However, before long, rain came and prevented any further decision.

In July, Statham experienced an unfortunate aspect of captaincy, when at Newark the Nottinghamshire supporters booed him for making a late declaration. On a boring last day, Lancashire's second innings indeed 'appeared over-cautious' to *Wisden*, who also thought the subsequent target set for Notts was 'unrealistic'. If Statham had been influenced by his side's fragile batting, that was no consolation for the crowd. Happily for Lancashire, their next match was a success for both the captain and his team.

This was against Hampshire at Old Trafford. The visitors began well by scoring 194 for 6 in their 65 overs and, thanks to Shackleton's 6 for 25, dismissing Lancashire for 97. The pitch had not yet been of particular benefit to the bowlers but it was now starting to wear. Hampshire began their second innings on the Monday at about 12.45pm. Marshall hooked and drove Statham for four, but he then fell to Higgs. At 11, the captain dismissed Reed and Gray with successive balls, and at lunch Hampshire were 30 for 3. The afternoon was so successful for Lancashire that the visitors were all out for 83, even though Lever was absent ill for most of the time.

Statham's contribution was to account for top-scorer Horton, well caught by Knox, and four late batsmen. Timms and Wheatley were each leg-before for ducks; nor did Shackleton, well caught by Worsley, or White stay long. Three times in the innings, Statham had taken two wickets in an over, and his final analysis was 14-5-24-7. *The Guardian* said that he had bowled with much of his old hostility and had varied his pace and swing cleverly. With the pitch wearing and with Shackleton to contend with (he bowled 45 overs for 32 runs), Lancashire took no risks in reaching 181 to win.

The following day, Lancashire played at Edgbaston, where the pitch, said *Wisden*, 'might have been prepared with Statham specially in mind'. It was green and moist early on, encouraging sharp deviation, and its pace and bounce varied. So Statham and Higgs, particularly, were on to a good thing.

Former Lancashire captain Bob Barber opened the Warwickshire batting. He was, said Statham, "bristling with intentions of slamming Ken Higgs and myself all over the Edgbaston ground," and he scored seven off Statham's first over. However, he edged his second attempted off drive against the same bowler and was caught at slip. After half an hour, with Higgs dismissing Abberley and Amiss and Statham making Mike Smith play on, the home team were 16 for 4.

The middle-order effected a slow recovery, and by early afternoon Warwickshire had reached 81 for 5. Then Higgs bowled Ibadulla, and Statham polished off the innings by taking the last four wickets in ten balls. He bowled Cartwright (the top scorer) and Miller in the same over, and in his next he dismissed Alan Smith and, first ball, Bannister. Warwickshire were thus all out for 84, Statham's analysis being 18.5-7-31-6. Lancashire, on a drier pitch, followed with a good score but in the end they were denied, by Barber and Amiss and by stoppages for rain, the victory which *Wisden* thought they deserved.

Statham took eight wickets in the match when Lancashire won at Chesterfield in July, and he took ten wickets during his county's sixth and last win, in late August. This was at Dover, where he was mainly responsible firstly for putting Kent in, and secondly for putting them out again. The pitch seemed green and moist, and indeed proved lively. But only after lunch, taken when Kent were 87 for 3, did Statham and Higgs cause a collapse. In the morning, which had begun with Luckhurst falling to a fine catch by Goodwin off Statham, Lever had met with the most success, by accounting for Cowdrey and Denness.

Shortly after the interval, Statham took two wickets in four balls: Wilson was bowled while trying to glance and then Ealham played on. Higgs took the next two wickets, to make the score 120 for 7. At the same total, Statham bowled Dixon and had Sayer lbw, and two runs later he ended the innings by knocking Graham's off stump flat. Since lunch, he had taken 5 for 14 (four of them bowled) giving him 6 for 32 in the innings. Lancashire went on to win a low-scoring match by four wickets.

In his final game of the summer, a rain-spoilt match against Surrey at Old Trafford, Statham completed his hundred wickets in a season for the 13th time. This is the most by a Lancashire bowler, the previous best being 12 times by Johnny Briggs. And Statham was again in 1966, as he had been the season before, third in the national averages as well as top of his county's list.

As for his leadership, the Committee reported that they 'had no hesitation in inviting him to captain the side in 1967 and were indeed pleased when the invitation was accepted'.

"What Record?"

IN May of this late-starting summer of 1967, all nine of Lancashire's fixtures were affected by rain, the last three being abandoned without a ball bowled. And for Statham and his co-bowlers, the season started inauspiciously in another respect.

They were on the receiving end of 22 fours hit by a 20-year-old on his Championship debut. This was at Hove, on a very cold day, just after Lancashire's match at Edgbaston had been interrupted by snow. But even in South African sunshine, Tony Greig could hardly have done better than score 156 in under four hours, and this innings helped to make him the Young Cricketer of the Year.

When he came out to bat Sussex were 34 for 3; Statham had claimed two of those wickets, but Greig, taking risks which came off, was 'particularly severe' on him, according to the *Manchester Evening News*. For example, he straight drove the Lancashire captain for four twice in one over, once off the front foot and once off the back foot. Higgs, Lever and Savage also suffered; Greig reached his century in three hours and then added 56 at a run-a-minute. By the time Savage trapped Greig at 270 for 6, Statham's figures had drifted from 2 for 15 to 2 for 60.

However, the captain improved matters by bowling the next three men, though Sussex took their total to 324. Statham finished with 27-9-70-5, which improvement *The Guardian* called 'a tribute to his spirit as well as to his stamina'. But because John Snow reduced Lancashire to 21 for 4 before the close, probably neither Statham nor his team objected to the rain which washed out the next two days' play.

Rain also dominated Lancashire's next match, against Worcestershire at Old Trafford, but not before Statham had shown his paces. On the first morning, the pitch was green and moist, and after Statham had Kenyon missed at slip, he trapped him leg-before with a break-back. Then he produced a nasty lifter which had Headley caught at point, and Higgs soon dismissed Ormrod. Graveney and D'Oliveira, though they were unable to score for 20 minutes, took the visitors to 74 for 3 at lunch.

D'Oliveira's first ball from Statham after the interval bowled him, but Graveney went on to make the top score of 51. However, even though he was described as in form and looking for runs, this took him three hours and contained only two fours. *Wisden* called his innings an interesting duel with Statham and Higgs. The captain later bowled the last two men, for an analysis of 20.4-6-37-5; Higgs had taken the other five in Worcester's 158 all out. Lancashire gained first-innings points but rain prevented any further decision.

At Old Trafford, starting on 21 June, against Nottinghamshire, came Lancashire's first victory of the season. The two first innings occupied two days, and Lancashire then declared overnight, having just won first-innings points. So the visitors began their second innings at the start of play on the last morning.

Statham bowled the first over, and his second ball, lifting slightly, had Norman Hill caught at the wicket. His sixth ball reared off a good length, and went off Bolus' bat and glove to Wood at short leg. Notts had thus lost both openers for ducks to Statham — who in the process had broken a Lancashire record that had stood since 1900.

But the *Manchester Evening News* said that at the time this went virtually unnoticed, adding that none of the players realized, and that there was no extra applause from the members' pavilion. In fact, the report ran, even Statham did not know. When asked for a comment, he said: "What record?"

The record was the number of wickets taken for Lancashire, and was previously 1,688 by Johnny Briggs. Only the season before, Statham had written: "The record book is something that never really interests me in cricket," which was a comment typical of the impression he gave throughout his career.

During the afternoon's play, though, the Lancashire secretary announced that the county were to mount the ball with an inscription in honour of the occasion and present it to Statham. And it was available at 2.30pm, because by then Notts were all out — for 86, with Statham and Higgs each taking 4 for 24. This meant that Lancashire needed a leisurely 84 to win, and in spite of a bad start they made it. So for the home captain, success had followed success all day.

August was a good month for Statham because Lancashire won three Championship matches and the bowler thrice took five wickets in an innings — though, as it happened, not in any of the victories. Statham began the month by taking 6 for 58 including the wickets of Milburn, Steele and Mushtaq, in helping his county to first-innings points against Northamptonshire. The next match was the Roses game at Bramall Lane. On the Saturday, Lancashire struggled to 183 all out on a green pitch, and late in the day Statham bowled the first over of Yorkshire's innings. His second ball whipped fatally into Boycott's shuffling pads, and his next two deliveries 'left Padgett's forward shot cleaving fresh air', said *The Guardian.* But Yorkshire reached 30 for 1 by the close.

On the Bank Holiday Monday, the crowd, disappointingly, was only 7,000. At 48, Statham had Padgett caught at the wicket, and at 70 he beat Ken Taylor completely with a ball which, moving away, just missed everything. Next ball, Taylor drove and missed, and was bowled middle stump. When Wood bowled Hampshire, the home side were 74 for 4.

Close led the Yorkshire resistance, though after lunch Statham as a fielder treated him generously! Once he fumbled Pilling's return which might have run Close out, and once he was unable to get to a possible mid-on catch off Higgs' bowling. Close reached his 50, despite losing partners, and at tea Yorkshire, with 184 for 7, had gained the lead. After the interval, Barry Wood had Close caught, and Statham bowled Binks and Nicholson: 207 all out, Statham's analysis being 26.4-4-82-5. On the last day, although Lancashire declared, a result was never likely because the two first innings had used up so much time.

Later in August, came Lancashire's winning streak, though Statham's most successful bowling during that period was in a match narrowly lost. This was at Worcester, where in the home side's second innings, he dismissed, albeit in bad light, three middle-order batsmen while conceding two runs. On the final morning he collected two more victims to finish with 18-7-27-5, whereas his figures had once read 0 for 18. But Lancashire failed by 17 runs to reach their winning target.

Thus, with their late run, Lancashire finished 11th in the table, one place higher than in 1966. They won only four Championship games but, on the other hand, they lost only three. It was that sort of season for most counties. There was a very high proportion of draws, partly because of the bad weather and partly because of a new scoring system which awarded four points for first-innings lead but only eight points for a win. And thirdly, in Lancashire's case, because many matches were saved by the players' 'new fighting spirit', as their loyal Committee reported.

They also reported that Statham 'again set an inspiring example as captain, bowling with his usual accuracy and hostility to finish tenth in the national averages, which at the age of 37 was a remarkable achievement'. So they seemed satisfied by the county's climb of one place in the table for the third consecutive year under Statham. He later wrote that he regarded this progress "as more significant than reaching the heights one season and plunging to the depths the next as so many counties do." And the success which Lancashire were to meet in the subsequent few seasons suggests that this was a sound assessment.

On the not-so-bright side, Statham's captaincy in 1967 'often puzzled', according to *Wisden's* Lancashire correspondent. And in this year too, the bowler's long sequence of taking a hundred wickets in a season, and also of topping the county's first-class averages, both came to an end. The former sequence was ten consecutive seasons, and the latter was 16.

But neither failure nor success, neither criticism nor praise, could alter the fact of Statham's age, which was as mentioned above by the Committee. He was now beyond the age at which many fast bowlers have retired from the first-class game; and he was nearing that at which the durable Lindwall and McDonald did so. The future which beckoned him was not fast bowling.

Calling it a Day

'EVERY member will be extremely sorry to have heard that Brian Statham has found it necessary to relinquish the captaincy which he has held for the last three years, and the Committee are very grateful for all he has done to help the Club during this most difficult period, the results of which are only just beginning to show. However, it is hoped that he will be able to continue playing for the County as long as he can, if only in occasional matches. In the meantime, the Committee wish to express their appreciation for all he has done and to wish him every possible success in his new venture.'

So said the Committee's report prepared during the close season of 1967-8. The new venture was a job as a brewery representative.

John Kay described the development thus: "Statham was invited to continue as captain in 1968 but, offered a business appointment to commence at the end of that summer, expressed a desire to stand down and play alongside a new captain." The new man was Jack Bond. Bond requested the appointment of Higgs as senior professional to help him — he knew there would be plenty of hard work, just as Statham had known. The latter wrote of his own time as captain: "Occasional victories have brought pleasure but for the main part it has been quite a task helping to rebuild the side that suffered badly through the departure of leading players, injuries and Test Match demands."

At first, Statham said he intended to finish cricket in July — when he was going on an unaccustomed summer holiday — but in fact he decided that his last game would be the Roses match at Old Trafford on 3 August, which was Ken Higgs' Benefit match.

Before the season began, Statham (with other former England players such as Trueman, Subba Row and Wardle) flew to Bombay in April, to play in a fixture to raise funds for local flood victims. The disaster area was about 150 miles south of Bombay, at Koyna, and Statham appeared for the President's XI, taking one wicket against the Prime Minister's XI.

Back in England, the weather was as bad as in 1967 for the start of the season. Nor were there many bright spells later on. Lancashire certainly brightened however: it was mid-June before they won a game, but they finished strongly and, with eight victories, secured sixth place in the table. Only Yorkshire gained more bowling points than Lancashire under the new bonus points system. Higgs took over a hundred wickets, while Shuttleworth, enjoying better fitness this season than Lever, helped to give the county hope that Statham's place could be filled.

In May, Statham made his final appearance at his favourite ground, Lord's. Following Bond's lunchtime declaration on the last day, Middlesex needed 267 to win in 230 minutes. Statham opened from the Pavilion End to Eric Russell, who drove, turned and pulled his first three balls for 2 fours and a three. However, Statham bowled him in his next over. The innings ticked along to 111 for 4 at tea, when the match looked a certain draw. But Statham changed that.

Operating now from the Nursery End, he bowled Titmus (at 122 for 5), and quickly had John Murray leg-before for a duck and Mike Smith caught by the newly-signed Engineer. He had taken these three wickets in ten balls without cost, and Middlesex were 125 for 7. He had Latchman leg-before at 135, and this after-tea spell finally read 11-6-13-4. But Hooker and Herman stayed together for an hour and though a tired Statham returned and bowled Herman, Middlesex survived with their last pair together.

Statham's analysis in the innings of 162 for 9 was 20-8-48-6. And in the process, he had broken another Lancashire bowling record, beating Johnny Briggs' total of 2,201 wickets in first-class cricket. Russell was in fact the record-breaking wicket, though at the time Titmus might have been so regarded. The doubt which arose concerned the status of Statham's one wicket in the Bombay match, which in the end was called first-class.

The return match against Middlesex in June turned out to be Lancashire's first win of the summer. In hot weather, the visitors started the last day, which was Statham's 38th birthday, at 14 for 0, on the way to erasing Lancashire's first-innings lead of 51. In achieving that, Middlesex lost three wickets, one of them to Statham who had Smith caught in the gully. However, a run-a-minute partnership between Radley and Titmus took the score to 141 for 3 before Statham struck in his afternoon spell.

He had Radley well caught by Engineer, Titmus caught at slip, and he bowled Latchman. This was in the space of 17 balls for two runs; and Middlesex, with Savage having bowled Murray, had collapsed to 148 for 7. After Hooker and Herman had often played at him and missed, Statham rested, his spell reading 8-3-5-3. His innings analysis, when the visitors were all out for 185, was 19-9-14-4. Lancashire reached their target in the final over.

At the end of June, Sussex visited Old Trafford, and fared badly at Statham's hands on the first morning. On a damp pitch, and in doubtful light which finally caused lunch to be taken ten minutes early, Statham bowled unchanged for about an hour and 40 minutes. At 28, he bowled Mike Buss; at 52, Suttle hooked a short ball and was caught on the long-leg boundary; at 55, Greig was well taken by the wicketkeeper off a ball which lifted. When, at 62, Oakman paid the penalty for a poor shot, Statham had taken all four wickets for 19 runs. After bowling 12 overs, he was rested. Subsequently, Shuttleworth was the spearhead, Statham's afternoon spell, 'surprisingly' said *The Guardian*, being ineffective. Sussex made 169, Lancashire tied on first innings, but the last day was rained off.

In late July, Statham missed two Championship games while he took his holiday, but he was ready for the Roses match on Saturday, 3 August. He replaced Lever, who had nevertheless bowled well during Statham's absence.

Of course Statham's finale would boost the prospects for Ken Higgs in the latter's Benefit match. Indeed, the senior player, now interrupting his first summer holiday for 18 years, said: "If I can help draw a bigger crowd than usual to Old Trafford for Ken's sake, it will be a pleasure. He has meant so much to me these last few years." The beneficiary, for his part, said of Statham: "I owe almost everything to him. He has helped me at all times and never failed to put me on the right path when out of touch." And he added: "I know where to go for the best advice."

Higgs' tribute was perhaps the closest to home, so to speak, but there were numerous others from further afield reported on the eve of Statham's last match. Colin Cowdrey said of him: "As an opponent, I can vouch for his remarkable ability to make you play every ball," while Trevor Bailey commented: "His deadly accuracy often astounded me." Sir Len Hutton claimed: "I knew how valuable he was and his figures, extraordinary as they are, do not do him justice."

Sir Learie Constantine's message was: "I cannot recall any other bowler who could combine so much ability with so placid a temperament." Freddie Brown, who had managed the MCC team in Australia in 1958-9, said: "He was always a trier and never a grouser. When he could not get them out himself, he softened them up for others. I know of nobody in cricket who would say a harsh word about him."

John Kay of the *Manchester Evening News* wrote: "And now he is going they can break the mould, for he has proved that really great fast bowlers are born and not made for the job." And: "Club officials, from Lord's to Old Trafford and back again, will tell you that, apart from a certain habit of forgetfulness, they never had an easier man to deal with than George." ('George' was a nickname which Statham happened to take over from Winston Place in 1955, the Lancashire team having a tradition of so dubbing one of its players).

The newspaper also quoted an interview with the bowler himself about his career. He said the match he would remember above all others was the 1950 Roses game (in which his performance did so much to get his career off the ground). The player whom he remembered most of all was Godfrey Evans (an extrovert, almost opposite in character to Statham). The batsman who had given him most trouble was, he said, Peter May.

The bowler he most admired: Fred Trueman. "He has the lot; pace, swing, temper and guts, and together we have had a wonderful time." (Regarding pace, incidentally, Statham thought that his partner was 'a shade quicker' than himself).

So we come to the Saturday of the farewell game itself. Higgs, because it was his Benefit match, was granted the tossing of the coin, and the outcome was that, in promising weather, Bond chose to bat. However, the crowd — 5,000 at the start and towards 10,000 after lunch — saw Lancashire struggle. When Bond went out to bat at number-four, he was loudly cheered, because his team had won five out of six Championship matches since their previous appearance at headquarters! But Lancashire were 124 for 8 when Statham's turn to bat arrived. He was given a standing ovation all the way to the wicket — where Trueman was in mid-over.

The batsman recalls that the bowler called across: "I'm having none of this sentimental nonsense. You're not getting any favours from me just because you're packing up." But (despite a scowling face and an extra-long run!), Trueman bowled a slow full toss and Statham duly got off the mark. He scored three before he was bowled by Hutton and applauded all the way back to the pavilion again. When the home side were all out for 162, Yorkshire were left with 80 minutes' batting before close of play.

According to one report, the pitch was easy-paced in the morning, but according to *Wisden* it now encouraged the Lancashire pace bowlers.

Statham, from the Stretford end, began by conceding a boundary to Sharpe for a confident square cut. Then came his second over. The second ball clean bowled Leadbeater and the sixth ball trapped Sharpe lbw. When Higgs dismissed Padgett, Yorkshire were 8 for 3. Statham in his third over had Hampshire leg-before, his third wicket in ten balls. And Higgs bowled Close to make the Champions 12 for 5!

It was left to Binks to improve his team's total to 32 before he lost Illingworth, caught in the gully by Higgs during Statham's eighth over. In his next over the same bowler sent Binks' off stump flying: 33 for 7. And, still in bright weather, the day's play ended with the run out of Trueman by David Hughes, the score-card reading:

	Yorkshire	
P.J.Sharpe	lbw b Statham	5
B.Leadbeater	b Statham	2
D.E.V.Padgett	c Engineer b Higgs	1
J.H.Hampshire	lbw b Statham	4
D.B.Close	b Higgs	0
R.Illingworth	c Higgs b Statham	1
J.G.Binks	b Statham	19
R.A.Hutton	not out	0
F.S.Trueman	run out	1
Extra		1
Total	**(8 wickets)**	**34**

Statham's contribution read 9.2-2-20-5.

The match was scheduled to continue the next afternoon — a Sunday; the John Player League (which Statham personally did not fancy) was planned to start the following year.

When the gates were opened on the Sunday for the Roses game, 'the rush was like the January sales', said *The Guardian*. In glorious sunshine, the attendance finally reached 21,659, the biggest for a county match at Old Trafford since the 1960 Roses fixture. One of the attractions now was Yorkshire's predicament!

In Statham's first full over of the day, he bowled Don Wilson, splaying the middle and off stump: 38 for 9. This was just what the home supporters were hoping to see. But they then had to endure 14 runs by last man Nicholson who was beaten by Statham around off stump perhaps a dozen times. When Nicholson was run out, Yorkshire had totalled 61, and Statham had bowled throughout the innings for an analysis of 17.5-4-34-6.

In their second innings, which they began with a lead of 101 in the bank, Lancashire disappointed the huge crowd. Though Wood scored 55, the home side were only 126 for 8 when Statham came out in the evening for his last innings in first-class cricket. He waved his bat to acknowledge the rapturous welcome he was given and chatted briefly with the Yorkshire wicketkeeper — who caught him off Wilson for a duck. Statham was applauded all the way back by Lancastrians and Yorkshiremen alike. So Lancashire finished this second day at 126 for 9; they were 227 ahead, but had they let Yorkshire off the hook?

On the Bank Holiday Monday the weather was pleasant but not as sunny as on the day before. Nearly 10,000 people arrived to see the finale, so the match had attracted, including members, over 40,000 spectators, of whom 29,644 were paying customers. The latter total easily exceeded that for Lancashire's entire 1966 home season of 15 fixtures. Admittedly this particular match had various ingredients which made it popular. But the moral was there and was to be often proved in the coming few years: people — in their leisure-time and especially on a Sunday — will come and watch a successful team. Fine weather helps, of course!

The crowd, over the three days, gave £1,100 to collections for Ken Higgs' Benefit, and although the county no longer granted a player a share of the gate money, the grand total for his Benefit season eventually reached £8,390. *The Guardian's* reporter was confident that Higgs, in his ten-year career, had earned every halfpenny of it.

So Lancashire started this Monday, the last day of Statham's first-class career, with plenty of support for, and interest in, their attempt to beat Yorkshire for the first time since 1960. A last-wicket stand between Higgs and Savage meant that towards noon, the visitors, top of the Championship table, set out to score 253 to win in 310 minutes.

Brian Close decided to open the batting with Sharpe, who soon off drove Statham for four. The bowler saw fit to retaliate. Firstly, he made Sharpe, on 16, snick a ball to first slip — but Shuttleworth put the catch down. Then, a few runs later, Statham trapped the same batsman very much leg-before, and umpire Syd Buller completed the formalities.

When Yorkshire were 69 for 3, one wicket having fallen to each pace bowler, Lancashire were on top, but Close and Illingworth restored the balance during the afternoon. Statham seemed tired at this stage 'but he alone did not partake of the mid-session drinks', said *The Guardian.* His first ball after this break was turned by Close to short square leg; but Wood missed an important chance. Shortly before tea, Hughes dismissed Illingworth (at 148 for 4), and on the stroke of the interval, Higgs accounted for Leadbeater: 159 for 5, with Close 70 not out.

At tea, 25 minutes' play plus the statutory 20 overs remained, for Yorkshire to score 94 more runs or for Lancashire to take five more wickets. Of course, a draw was on the cards, and after Don Wilson had made a brief attempt to go for the runs, Close decided his team's task was too much. At five o'clock, they required 80 runs from the final 20 overs, which were begun by Higgs and Shuttleworth. All the pace had gone from the pitch, but Higgs beat Wilson, albeit to no avail. A draw, especially with Shuttleworth not bowling well, became more and more likely.

Statham came on at about 5.15pm from the Warwick Road End. Bowling very straight, he sent down five maidens in a row. *The Times* thought that 'watching him do so, no one could have doubted that there are still hundreds of wickets left in him which, if he wished, he could add to the 2,260 he has taken'.

At about ten minutes to six, Statham bowled his final ball in first-class cricket — it was on a good length and on the middle stump.

There were six overs still available, but Jack Bond decided that it was beyond Lancashire to win. So he called a halt, whereupon Close shook Statham's hand. The bowler collected his cap and sweater from umpire George Pope, and turned for the pavilion for the last time.

His route was encroached upon by a swarm of youngsters, with a few policemen here and there in case of need. Ten Lancashire fielders and the two batsmen milled around in the wings, knowing that the stage belonged to Statham. Everyone, including the Yorkshire players on the balcony, joined in the standing ovation which he received as he led the way off the field.

So, walking slowly but surely to the pavilion gate, he left his playing days behind him.

Statham Statistics

BOWLING FIGURES

All First-Class Matches

	Matches	Overs	Mdns	Runs	Wkts	Ave
1950	15	300.5	82	613	37	16.56
1950-51 in Australia	2	*36	6	109	3	36.33
1950-51 in New Zealand	3	54	13	111	8	13.87
1951	27	714.2	178	1466	97	15.11
1951-52 in India & Pakistan	15	369.5	106	807	40	20.17
1952	28	881.4	186	1989	110	18.08
1953	28	723.1	229	1650	101	16.33
1953-54 in West Indies	5	194.5	35	541	22	24.59
1954	22	615.3	194	1300	92	14.13
1954-55 in Australia	10	*244.3	40	778	38	20.47
1954-55 in New Zealand	3	82.2	30	138	16	8.62
1955	22	754.5	216	1573	108	14.56
1956	25	679.3	210	1351	91	14.84
1956-57 in South Africa	12	*233.2	40	607	36	16.86
1957	28	896.4	251	1895	126	15.03
1958	29	893.3	275	1648	134	12.29
1958-59 in Australia	9	*209.1	30	549	28	19.60
1959	26	977.4	267	2087	139	15.01
1959-60 in West Indies	6	213	57	493	15	32.86
1960	27	844.1	274	1662	135	12.31
1960-61 in South Africa	4	97.3	24	240	21	11.42
1961	28	1024.2	309	2107	104	20.25
1962	28	947.2	221	2207	102	21.63
1962-63 in Australia	9	*290.5	34	1043	33	31.60
1963	25	791	168	1874	113	16.58
1964	29	881.4	170	2203	110	20.02
1965	24	771	205	1716	137	12.52
1966	25	624.4	134	1479	102	14.50
1967	24	635.2	156	1530	92	16.63
1967-68 in India	1	12	0	50	1	50.00
1968	20	489	124	1179	69	17.08
Totals	559	100,925 balls	4264	36,995	2,260	16.36

*8-ball overs

Test Matches

	Opponents	Tests	Overs	Mdns	Runs	Wkts	Ave
1950-51	New Zealand	1	24	6	47	1	47.00
1951	South Africa	2	48	14	78	4	19.50
1951-52	India	5	126	36	293	8	36.62
1953	Australia	1	43	10	88	2	44.00
1953-54	West Indies	4	153	24	460	16	28.75
1954	Pakistan	4	89	26	213	11	19.36
1954-55	Australia	5	*143.3	16	499	18	27.72
1954-55	New Zealand	2	58.4	24	91	12	7.58
1955	South Africa	4	177.2	54	363	17	21.35
1956	Australia	3	106	35	184	7	26.28
1956-57	South Africa	4	*130.1	20	349	14	24.92
1957	West Indies	3	158.1	37	433	13	33.30
1958	New Zealand	2	67	20	130	7	18.57
1958-59	Australia	4	*104	12	286	12	23.83
1959	India	3	112.2	44	223	17	13.11
1959-60	West Indies	3	130.4	42	286	10	28.60
1960	South Africa	5	203	54	491	27	18.18
1961	Australia	4	201.4	41	501	17	29.47
1962	Pakistan	3	120.1	40	278	16	17.37
1962-63	Australia	5	*165.2	16	580	13	44.61
1963	West Indies	2	81	10	243	3	81.00
1965	South Africa	1	53.2	12	145	7	20.71
	Totals	70	16,056 balls	593	6,261	252	24.84

*8-ball overs

All Lancashire Matches

	Matches	Overs	Mdns	Runs	Wkts	Ave
1950	15	300.5	82	613	37	16.56
1951	24	649.2	159	1358	92	14.76
1952	27	839.1	177	1886	107	17.62
1953	26	664.1	214	1526	97	15.73
1954	17	494.3	156	1016	78	13.02
1955	16	528.5	156	1077	84	12.82
1956	22	573.3	175	1167	84	13.89
1957	24	728.3	212	1431	112	12.77
1958	26	810.3	253	1459	125	11.67
1959	22	833.3	212	1800	115	15.65
1960	21	616.1	213	1131	106	10.66
1961	23	813.4	266	1580	87	18.16
1962	25	827.1	181	1929	86	22.43
1963	22	677	148	1560	104	15.00
1964	28	875.4	170	2178	109	19.98
1965	23	717.4	193	1571	130	12.08
1966	25	624.4	134	1479	102	14.50
1967	24	635.2	156	1530	92	16.63
1968	20	489	124	1179	69	17.08
Totals	430	12699.1	3381	27470	1816	15.12

J.B.Statham's Lancashire County Cricket Club Records

1. Most Tests for England: 70
(C.Washbrook: 37)

• • • • • • • • • • •

2. Most Test Wickets: 252
(S.F.Barnes: 189)

• • • • • • • • • • •

3. Most wickets in first-class cricket: 2,260
(J.Briggs: 2,221 formerly 2,201)

• • • • • • • • • • •

4. Most wickets for Lancashire: 1,816
(J.Briggs: 1,696 formerly 1,688)

• • • • • • • • • • •

5. 100 first-class wickets in a season: 13 times
(J.Briggs: 12 times)

• • • • • • • • • • •

6. Top of Lancashire CCC first-class averages in 16 seasons
(R.Tyldesley in 8 seasons)

• • • • • • • • • • •

7. Cheapest 100 wickets for Lancashire: average 10.66 in 1960
(J.Briggs: average 11.57 in 1888)

Bibliography

Arlott, J. *Fred* (Eyre and Spottiswoode 1971)
Arlott, J. *The Great Bowlers* (Pelham Books 1968)
Bailey, T. *The Greatest of My Time* (Eyre and Spottiswoode 1968)
Bailey, T. and Trueman, F. *From Larwood to Lillee* (Queen Anne Press 1984)
Cardus, N. *Close of Play* (Collins 1956)
Cowdrey, M.C. *M.C.C. The Autobiography of a Cricketer* (Hodder and Stoughton 1976)
Dexter, E. (Editor) *Rothmans Book of Test Matches, England v Australia, 1946-1963* (Arthur Barker 1964)
Hutton, L. *Just My Story* (Hutchinson 1956)
Kay, J. *History of County Cricket: Lancashire* (Arthur Barker 1972)
Lancashire County C.C. Year Books.
Marshall, J. *Old Trafford* (Pelham Books 1971)
Peebles, I. *Bowler's Turn* (Souvenir Press 1960)
Statham, J.B. *Cricket Merry-Go-Round* (Stanley Paul 1956)
Statham, J.B.*Flying Bails* (Stanley Paul 1961)
Statham, J.B. *A Spell at the Top* (Souvenir Press 1969)
Statham, J.B. and Graveney, T. *Instructions to Young Cricketers* (Museum Press 1955)
Swanton, E.W. *West Indies Revisited* (Heinemann 1960)
Thomson, A.A. *Cricket: The Golden Ages* (Stanley Paul 1961)
Thomson, A.A. *The Wars of the Roses* (Pelham Books 1967)
Tyson, F. *A Typhoon Called Tyson* (Heinemann 1961)
Wisden Cricketers' Almanacks.

Index
(of Test players and Lancashire players)